COMMAND
VERSUS DEMAND
Systems for Economic Growth

Edited with Introductions by
SHANTI S. TANGRI
WAYNE STATE UNIVERSITY

D. C. HEATH AND COMPANY · BOSTON

CONTENTS

III. COMMAND VERSUS DEMAND: PRICES, PROFITS, AND PLANNING

IV. COMMAND VERSUS DEMAND: PROSPECTS FOR CONVERGENCE

INTRODUCTION

All economic systems share some ends and means for attaining those ends, though the emphasis placed on the attainment of different ends and the use of different means varies in different systems — indeed in different economies within each system. If systems had nothing in common, it would be meaningless to compare them.[1] One of the common goals of all contemporary systems is economic growth. Two of the common mechanisms for achieving growth are the forces of market demand and of political command or authority. The readings in this volume focus on economic systems in which most of the crucial economic decisions for achieving economic growth are made through either command or demand mechanisms.

The nature and pace of economic growth depends considerably on how a society answers the questions that face all societies: what to produce? how much? for whom? and how? The questions can be answered in three ways:[2]

1) by following the dictates of a single individual — a king, a general, a commissar, a patriarch, or a priest — or a small group of people — a military junta, a party committee, an oligarchy of wealth or old families;
2) by following the dictates of all the individuals and groups in or outside the geographical or political boundaries of the community who enter the market as buyers and suppliers of goods and services;
3) by following the dictates of tradition and custom handed down from generation to generation.

While all systems use elements of all three mechanisms, systems can be

[1] See Carl Landauer, *Contemporary Economic Systems* (Philadelphia, 1964), pp. 6–11, 17–23.

[2] Gregory Grossman, "Notes for a Theory of the Command Economy," *Soviet Studies*, Vol. XV; No. 2 (October 1963), pp. 101–123; and Robert L. Heilbroner, *The Making of Economic Society* (Englewood Cliffs, N. J., 1962), pp. 9–17.

classified according to the mechanism employed most: command, demand, or tradition.

The traditional system is not well suited to the task of economic change. If "what was good enough for Jonah is good enough for me" is a basic tenet of belief in a society, it is unlikely, by its own efforts, to achieve a standard of living much above that of Jonah.

Communist nations rely largely on command mechanisms. Demand plays a role in these economies but at the behest of the power elite who stand ready to restore the hegemony of command mechanisms. If they permit market forces to operate in vast areas of the economy for a generation or more it might not be easy to restore command mechanisms; but that is conjecture. Meanwhile, even significant decentralization, as in Yugoslavia since 1957 or in Czechoslovakia since 1962, does not amount to complete autonomy of consumers and producers since it constitutes delegation of powers which can be withdrawn.

Influenced by the writings of classical economists and Utilitarian Radicals of the eighteenth and nineteenth century, such as Adam Smith and John Stuart Mill, economists (and large numbers of laymen in the West) had come to believe that individual liberty is a necessary and often a sufficient condition for economic growth; conversely slavery, in any form, is an inefficient economic institution. Some economists, such as Von Mises, went on to theorize that a command economy in which individuals and private groups could not own property and buy and sell their material and nonmaterial resources (land, labor, and capital) would have no genuine economic markets.[3] Consequently, they reasoned, production units would have no idea of the real (opportunity) costs of inputs or values of outputs, or, as Hayek argued, it would be extremely difficult to find these costs and values in practice even if these could be computed in theory.[4] Hence, efficient rational resource allocation (microstatic efficiency) would be impossible in such economies. This in turn meant, many believed, little or no growth in the economy (macrodynamic inefficiency). Such neoclassical thought ignored or was unaware of the gains a command system could obtain from full, or fuller, employment of its resources (macrostatic efficiency).[5]

The early dislocation of the Soviet economy under War Communism

[3] Ludwig Von Mises, "Economic Calculation in the Socialist Commonwealth," in *Collectivist Economic Planning,* ed. F. A. Von Hayek (London, 1935), pp. 87–130.

[4] F. A. Von Hayek, "The Present State of the Debate," in *Collectivist Economic Planning.*

[5] John Maynard Keynes' writings, such as *The General Theory of Employment, Interest and Money* (New York, 1936), shifted the attention of economists from problems of resource allocation to the macro problems of resource utilization (full employment) and were only peripherally concerned with problems of growth. Joseph Schumpeter deviated from classical and neoclassical

and its consequent recovery during a partial return to capitalistic markets under the New Economic Policy in the 1920's lent support to such views. However, the rapid growth of the Soviet economy, under planning since 1928, has belied these expectations. Most economists now believe that a command economy can force the pace of development by full mobilization of its resources and by producing very high rates of investment (financed by forced savings) which could more than offset any decreases in output resulting from misallocation of resources, organizational inefficiency, and lack of adequate incentives for the mass of people. Soviet planning, it may be said, is inefficient microstatically, but efficient macrostatically and macrodynamically.

If the earlier view that a command system could not be efficient has been disproved by events and ideas it would be a mistake to go to the other extreme and assume that any command system, at any stage of development, is more efficient than a demand system. Many of the feudal and military command systems of the Middle East and Latin America are being used to sustain traditional ways of life inimical to change and growth. Command produces what the commander desires — change or stagnation. Communists inevitably, and military dictators occasionally, such as Kemal Ataturk in Turkey or Ayub Khan in Pakistan, intensely desire change and economic growth. Where a command system sustains and is sustained by a "universalistic" ideology and a monolithic party structure and cadres as under Communism or Nazism, it is more likely to achieve its goals than a command system based only on military power, "particularistic" value systems, and narrow interests of some families or clans.

If the system is totalitarian, *i.e.*, is controls social life in its totality, it is able to concentrate resources on a few chosen goals such as defense, space exploration, or heavy industry. Successes in a few selected areas may overshadow sluggishness or failure in neglected sectors. The politically distrusted and powerless peasantry is usually the segment of population which suffers the most in such systems and hence the agricultural sector performs poorly.

Authoritarian systems, such as some Latin military dictatorships, do not, by definition, have control over the complete social life of the community. Their capacity to marshal resources for achieving ends is more limited than that of totalitarian systems. However, this weakness may be

thought in recognizing that capitalism may operate with less than full employment for long periods of time, but he considered this a virtue: "A system — any system, economic or other — that at *every* point of time fully utilizes its possibilities to the best advantage may yet in the long run be inferior to a system that does so at *no* given point of time, because the latter's failure to do so may be a condition for the level or speed of its long run performance." *Capitalism, Socialism, and Democracy* (3rd ed.; New York, 1950), p. 83. John Kenneth Galbraith has developed this theme at some length in *American Capitalism: The Concept of Countervailing Power* (Boston, 1952).

more than offset by gains of productivity which result from the relative freedom and initiative of the peasantry and other productive groups. The authoritarian governments of Japan were more successful in generating agricultural progress by teaching the peasants better production methods than was Stalin's totalitarian regime.[6]

A command system may be quite efficient, as Arthur Lewis has pointed out, when the economy is simple, its goals are few (as during a war), the mass of people is ignorant and the chief knows better. The same command systems however may become very inefficient when the economy, as a result of growth, becomes complex and people more informed. The leadership then cannot know better than millions of reasonably informed consumers and producers.[7] Patterns of paternal care which make for healthy homes and growing children, if maintained beyond childhood, may produce rebellious adolescents or apathetic adults.

This indeed may be the lesson that the Russians are learning as their economy moves into a complex industrial society manned by skilled, urbanized, and educated workers and professionals. Furthermore, when there is a sufficient quantity of goods, quality becomes a paramount concern. Output is output only if the buyer wants it, otherwise it represents wasted resources. Buyers become increasingly more selective as economic growth progresses. With rising levels of income, therefore, the efficient allocation of resources for the production of goods in demand (microstatic efficiency) may indeed become a crucial condition for the continuation of rapid growth (macrodynamic efficiency).

Historically, capitalist economies have solved their economic problems largely as dictated by the changing patterns and volumes of market demand for various goods and services. While there has been a tendency to equate market demand with private demand (of consumers and producers), this is neither theoretically necessary nor historically correct. Governments in all capitalist systems have affected, and affect, the volume and composition of demand significantly. Traditionally government demand has been largely in the areas of defense, internal security, justice, and several other essential services with which the community could not be adequately supplied through the workings of the market mechanism. Japan represents perhaps the best example of activist governments which have used the market mechanism for transferring a feudal economy into a modern industrial economy. Japan has had perhaps the most rapid

[6] W. Arthur Lewis, *The Theory of Economic Growth* (Homewood, Ill., 1955), pp. 136, 188–89, 230–31, 244, 279, 388, 407. Moreover, it should be noted that the question of whether the command systems of the Russian and other Communist economies are logical derivatives of the Marxist-Leninist ideology or are the consequences of accident and historical circumstances is still a matter of considerable disagreement among historians, political scientists and economists.

[7] Lewis, *The Theory of Economic Growth,* pp. 80–84.

rates of growth of any country for almost a century. Most capitalist governments are increasingly expanding their role in controlling, regulating, and sustaining market forces.

Individuals and groups whose poverty prevents their needs from being translated into demand in economic markets have come to make their demands felt in political markets, especially where free voting and political competition have become well established. Fiscal and monetary policies for full employment, social security, health insurance, unemployment insurance, subsidized farming, education, and health care are some of the measures adopted to satisfy the demands articulated in political markets. Even nationalization reflects aspects of a demand system in a democratic community. Thus the voters, whose demand led to the nationalization of steel in postwar Britain, were able when their demand changed, to bring about denationalization of the industry. Economic and political markets complement and correct each other. The egalitarian political market (one man, one vote) tends to temper the harsh results of the weighted voting of the economic markets (more money, more influence).

But even if one kept to the conventional meaning of demand, nationalization of industry need not mean suppression of the market. As Lange, Taylor, Lerner[8] and others have argued this may be a pattern for socialist economies in which consumers retain their sovereignty while a planning board sets prices (and only prices) to clear the markets. Yugoslavia was the first Communist country to introduce significant features of such a model of market socialism. Czechoslovakia has plunged headlong into a variant of this system recently. Other Eastern European economies are debating the issues and are experimenting piecemeal with market demand and decentralization. The success of Yugoslavia, which a decade ago could certainly have been classified as underdeveloped, suggests that centralized planning of the Russian variety need not be the best system even for a poor country,[9] and that simple economies in which the chief knows best may be rarer than we think.

Just as the centrally planned economies are learning the value of market forces for improving their microstatic efficiency, the capitalist economies have been learning the value of aggregative planning for improving their macrostatic and macrodynamic efficiency. Capitalism in postwar Europe and post-Eisenhower America has experienced accelerated rates of economic growth just at the time when the command systems are

[8] Oskar Lange and Fred M. Taylor, *On the Economic Theory of Socialism,* ed. and with an introduction by Benjamin E. Lippincott (Minneapolis, 1938), McGraw-Hill 1961 paperback edition. Abba P. Lerner, *Economics of Control* (New York, 1944).

[9] See especially the discussion of the Yugoslavian economy in Rudolph Bićanic, "Economic Growth under Centralized and Decentralized Planning — A Case Study," *Economic Development and Cultural Change* (October 1957).

experiencing deceleration of their growth rates. Whether these new trends will continue in the future and the narrowing gap between the growth rates of command and demand systems will disappear or even reverse itself is still conjectural.

The increasing use of national planning policies in demand systems and of markets and market criteria in command systems could lead to convergence of the two systems in a purely technical sense. Whether that will diminish or intensify the competition between the two economic and political systems is a matter of debate.

That culture and folklore can be independent factors affecting economic growth of systems is corroborated by the slowness with which Americans have experimented with the budget as a stabilizing and expansionary tool and the Communists have approached the use of market prices and profits as instruments of economic policy.

It would be hazardous to make guesses about the future. At the moment, it appears both systems are learning how to rectify their internal deficiencies; which system will learn faster is hard to say. Both systems are in flux and systems, like men, usually learn from experience and change their goals with age and maturation. But not all social changes, Marx and Marxist doctrine notwithstanding, are predictable.

Purists often insist that all planning is coercive and inconsistent with a demand system[10] (or conversely that profit and interest are capitalistic evils which have no place in a socialist planned economy).[11] But planning and markets are consistent both with systems of demand and of command. If the people through their demand can introduce, modify and then eliminate planning, the system should be considered a demand system. It is centralized physical or quantitative planning which has shown itself to be inconsistent with a demand system. After all, some form of planning is necessary for any organized community. In any demand system, individual firms and local, state, and central governments need short- or long-run plans. Even a laissez-faire government, as Robbins has pointed out, needs to plan the legal and judicial framework of the economy very carefully.[12]

---

[10] The most forceful attack on planning is F. A. Von Hayek, *The Road to Serfdom* (Chicago, 1944). A variation on the theme is Milton Friedman, *Capitalism and Freedom* (Chicago, 1962).

[11] Most Marxists and many anti-Marxists have often confused the nature of interest, rents, and profits as prices for the proper allocation and use of scarce resources — capital, land, and entrepreneurial talent — with the economic desirability of paying out interest, rents, and profits to individuals and groups. The moral justification of these payments is yet another question which has only added to the voluminous and confusing literature. Recently Soviet economists have shown increasing awareness of these distinct issues. Polish economists have long treated these problems with theoretical astuteness and sophistication.

[12] Lionel Robbins, *Economic Planning and International Order* (London, 1937), esp. pp. 221–229 and 259–268.

Rapid economic growth has come to be an almost universally desired social objective especially since the Second World War. There is scarcely a politician in democratic or authoritarian societies who is willing to espouse slow growth, let alone no growth. Various reasons account for this.

Systems of national accounts may exaggerate the growth of real output by ignoring social and psychological costs of rapid change. Moreover, definitions of output are not completely free of value judgments or conventions. The Communist economies count only material output. Services, including those of the planners, have no value to be incorporated in national income accounts, but they add up the values of cottonseed, cotton, cotton fibre, cloth, and clothing. The total output, by this definition, is several times what it would be if the "value added" approach were used as in the United States or if a single family or firm were to carry out all the above operations in the Soviet Union. Increasing specialization, characterizing a growing economy can thus lead to the statistical illusion of rapid economic growth while the growth in value added may be much smaller.[13]

But there is "double counting" in non-Soviet economies also. New capital goods are part of current output and so are the goods produced with these capital goods in both types of economies. Thus wherever both the value of a new house and its rental income are counted in current output, there is some double counting.[14]

Services of the housewife are not included in gross national product anywhere. If she goes out to work for others, and her tasks are performed by laundries and restaurants and maids, the Gross National Product (GNP) goes up by the full value of the marketed services of the housewife and of those who take care of her work. Professor Pigou's famous example of the national income going down when a man marries his maid illustrates this problem. Economic growth is associated with increased participation of women in the labor force and increased monetization and commercialization of activities formerly carried on within the household or the farm. Some of the observed growth in income is thus simply a product of our accounting systems. Perhaps at very high levels of income, as in contemporary America, some of these trends are reversed;

[13] Abraham S. Becker, "Comparisons of the United States and USSR National Output: Some Rules of the Game," *World Politics* (October 1960). For a Soviet view see V. N. Starovskii, "On the Methodology of Comparing Economic Indices of the USSR and the USA," *Voprosy Ekonomiki*, 1960, No. 4, translated in *Problems of Economics* (July 1960), pp. 14–24.

[14] For a review of problems in the national income accounts of the U.S., see Gardner Ackley, *Macroeconomic Theory* (New York), pp. 38–90; for a more detailed treatment of U.S. and U.N. systems of such accounts see Richard and Nancy Ruggles, *National Income Accounts and Income Analysis* (2nd ed., New York, 1956), pp. 16–143.

more and more of a man's leisure is being turned into household work.[15] Some believe women are returning to the household. This may tend to slow down the rate of measured economic growth in mature economies. Similarly economic growth may make some daily necessities so abundant as to make them very cheap or even free goods, (such as cold drinking water and rest rooms in public places) which do not enter national income accounts. Our statistics, then, may underestimate true growth of output.

On the one hand growth has resulted in improved sanitary conditions and drinking water; on the other hand it has caused the pollution of air, lakes, and rivers and destroyed natural beauty and wildlife. Conservationists, poets, and philosophers have not been very successful in their protests against man's wanton destruction of nature in the name of progress. The glitter of growing wealth has usually tended to blind men to the growth of garbage that comes with more production and consumption.

Growth has come to dominate the minds of men, more rather than less, even as some of its adverse consequences have come to stir the imaginations of many people. The recent laws passed by the 89th U.S. Congress for conservation and beautification are small steps towards social reckoning of some of the costs of growth.

People living at subsistence levels do not have a life long enough or healthy enough to enjoy the beauty of nature; indeed, their environment may be ugly and bare. Conquering disease, filth, ugliness, hunger, and privation necessitates economic growth. Once the process of economic change becomes embedded in the attitudes and cultural and social institutions of a society, growth acquires a certain momentum of its own. The appetite for economic growth seems to feed upon itself.

Growth lifts the burden of back-breaking and noxious manual work from growing numbers of people. It frees women and other oppressed groups from the tyranny of tradition in male-dominated cultures.[16]

While growth causes some political and social tensions on balance it dissolves such tensions. It is easier to cut a "growing pie" more evenly than to cut a static pie more evenly. Similarly, growth permits a society's rival claims of defense, foreign aid, internal and social reform to be met with less social conflict.

Finally, in recent years, growth has become an international status symbol. Communists in particular have tried to make the growth rates of economies appear the single most important criterion of success of a social system.

[15] Tibor and Anne Scitovsky, "What Price Economic Progress?" *The Yale Review* (Autumn, 1959), pp. 95–110.

[16] For a general case advocating economic growth, see W. Arthur Lewis, "Is Economic Growth Desirable?" in *The Theory of Economic Growth*, pp. 420–35. For a sampling of views on the necessity for America to grow rapidly, see the contributions in *The Goal of Economic Growth*, ed. Edmund S. Phelps (New York, 1962), pp. 3–42.

Obviously "growth at any cost" is neither a communist nor a non-communist objective. No society is willing to sacrifice its internal or external security for the sake of more growth. The Soviet Union has perhaps only 2/5 of the U.S. GNP, a somewhat smaller fraction of U.S. per capita output. All the same, it devotes about the same proportion of GNP to defense.

No system can afford to let large numbers of its people starve to death for the sake of growth. But one system may be willing to put up with or even enforce starvation on some or semi-starvation on many of its people to attain the goals of its rulers, goals which may include rapid economic growth. Authoritarian societies have usually been successful in enforcing higher rates of saving and capital formation. Internalized discipline and loyalty to the culture and regime or externally enforced discipline have made populations give up as much as 40 per cent of the total output for purposes of saving and capital formation in Japan and many Communist countries. High rates of saving in both East and West Germany may be partly explained in similar terms.

Societies have other goals which often compete with growth. Full employment and maximum growth can under certain circumstances be in conflict. More equal distribution of income, better social welfare measures, greater regard for the individual's right to leisure, or a concern for aesthetic values may conflict with criteria of economic efficiency and growth.

A society, planned or unplanned, which puts a high value on these competing goals has to sacrifice some growth, while a society which pursues economic growth as an overriding objective is much more likely to achieve this goal, though at the cost of some other goals — at least for a generation or two until a large industrial and economic base permits it to become more diversified in the pursuit of its goals.

Even if different societies put the same emphasis on economic growth, the one that follows consumer preferences may not be able to progress as fast as one which selects its output composition otherwise.

FIGURE I

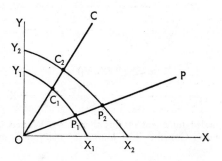

Figure 1 represents the production possibility curve $X_1 P_1 C_1 Y_1$ in a society which produces only the goods X and Y. Technological progress is more marked in the production of X than of Y so that in the next period of time, the production possibility curve shifts to $X_2 P_2 C_2 Y_2$. Any ray through the origin represents increasing quantities of X and Y in a fixed proportion. It is clear that growth along OP is faster than along OC since $\frac{P_1 P2}{OP_1} > \frac{OC_1}{C_1 C_2}$. Since technology reduces costs more for X than for Y, the planners may want to produce an output mix with as much X, and therefore as little Y, as feasible. Consumers on the other hand may want much more of Y and less of X, but respecting their wishes entails slower rates of growth.

Suppose now that Y represents food, housing, clothing, and other goods which consumers want while X represents the goods the planners or politicians prefer, such as engineering goods and metals in which technology produces relatively larger gains (represented by a greater shift of the production possibility curve along X than along Y). Suppose further that the planners do plan and achieve growth along OP. You then have the conditions of dissatisfied consumers in a rapidly growing economy. This may be a reasonable portrayal of many Communist economies.[17]

In real life, of course, economic growth alters the composition of output. Income elasticities of demand for various products vary with levels of income. Planners' ideological commitments (to steel, electricity, or anything else), or bureaucratic inflexibilities may rigidify patterns of output for long periods of time. Meanwhile, the patterns of consumer demand keep changing. Therefore, even if the planners had produced a pattern of output to match the pattern of demand initially, with time the supply and demand patterns get increasingly out of line, thus widening the gulf between what is needed and what is produced.

FIGURE 2

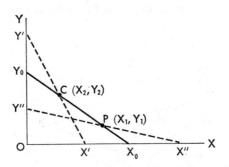

[17] For an extended treatment of this theme, see Warren G. Nutter, "On Measuring Economic Growth," *The Journal of Political Economy* (February 1957), pp. 51–63.

The changing pattern of output also creates problems in the measurement of output over time (the index number problem). Two bundles are exactly worth two times one bundle, as long as the bundles are alike. But the picture is fuzzy when the proportion of different goods in the bundles changes as the number of bundles grows.

Thus, in Figure 2, suppose one could buy, with a given budget, OXo of X or OYo of Y. It can be shown that all points on the straight line XoYo ("the budget line") represent combinations of X and Y that can be bought with this budget and are therefore equivalent. All points inside the line represent less value while all points outside the line represent higher value. The bundles P (representing amounts X_1 and Y_1) and C (representing X_2 and Y_2) are thus exactly equivalent if the outputs OXo and OYo are equal in value so that the slope of the line XoYo defines the price of one product in terms of the other.

But if the relative prices were to change to Y'X', then the bundle P will be worth more than the bundle C. Conversely if the relative prices were to change to Y''X'', then the bundle C would be worth more than the bundle P. In a dynamic situation relative prices do (and should) change. But the choice of relative prices of different years as weights for different components of the production index may yield very different output indices. The use of prices of earlier years gives too much weight to rapidly growing commodities (such as X). Because of scarcity, their prices in earlier years are very high. Use of current-year prices conversely tends to understate the magnitude of growth. But we can neither know the degree of overestimation nor of underestimation. The problem is theoretically insoluble. The widely held notion that Soviet GNP is a little less than half of the U.S. GNP was obtained by arbitrarily averaging two such estimates based on different relative prices: the one estimate put the ratio at 1/3; while the other was twice as much, i.e., 2/3.[18]

If all prices were to rise or fall proportionally due to monetary or fiscal mismanagement (or deliberately planned inflation or deflation) it is easy to adjust output indices so as to remove the effects of price changes. However, a general rise of prices invariably affects different sectors of the economy differently. Hence relative prices change during inflation or deflation, giving rise to the theoretically insoluble problems of measurement of output.

The problems are difficult enough for comparing output in two different periods within the same country. But when one compares economies with widely different climates, political systems and cultural values, the comparison loses more meaning.

If one adds to all this the problems caused by Communist secrecy

[18] Morris Bornstein, "A Comparison of Soviet and United States National Product," United States Congress, Joint Economic Committee, *Comparisons of the United States and Soviet Economies* (Washington, D. C., 1959), Part II, pp.377–95.

about statistics, especially in the past, and different definitions of gross output, it should be clear why serious students study comparative rates of growth with a healthy dose of skepticism.

But even if we assumed that patterns of demand and output and cultural values were similar in two systems, that we had no index number problems due to changing composition of output or due to changes in absolute or relative prices, and that the emphasis placed on various social goals — especially economic growth — were similar, it would still be difficult to attribute differences in the relative performance of two economies to the differences in their economic systems.

Accidents of leadership, good or bad weather, natural calamities, historical circumstances and many other unpredictable factors can accelerate or slow down economies for significant periods of time. The Communists, like others, but contrary to their deterministic ideology, use such events to explain the varying fortunes of their economies. However, the longer the period under study, the less the role of random events. Command economies have been in existence only for a fraction of the time for which demand economies have existed. Yet the period may be considered long enough for some tentative comparison.

These readings are focused on the varieties of command and demand systems and their effectiveness in generating economic *growth*. Systems for bringing about rapid economic *development* have been omitted. Bringing the latter into the picture raises additional issues concerning the optimal strategy of producing the social, cultural, and political changes which are concomitants or prerequisites of economic growth in poor countries. The lessons of growth may or may not be relevant for problems of development. China, for this reason, has been left out. Yugoslavia is a borderline case, while East Germany is an industrialized nation and has therefore been included.

The first section of the readings describes the contrasting and conflicting themes of command and demand as mechanisms for economic growth. The second section considers the varieties of patterns and performance of these systems. Section Three highlights the current debate about the changes needed in the role of prices and profits in command economies while the last section introduces conflicting viewpoints about the prospects for convergence between the two systems.

PART ONE

MECHANISMS AND THEORIES

INTRODUCTION

Most economists consider efficiency in resource allocation necessary, or at least helpful, in the attainment of economic growth. Allocational efficiency rests upon rational choice between alternative uses of scarce inputs for satisfying competing demands.

In the early postwar period a professor of economics, who became Minister of Economics and Chancellor of West Germany, tried to persuade his countrymen, fellow economists, and the Allied military governments in occupation of the necessity of using the market mechanism for rebuilding the war-shattered German economy. "The real contradistinction," he reasoned, "is not between free and planned economic systems, not between capitalist and socialist economic systems, but between a market economy with free price-level adjustment on the one hand and an authoritarian economy with state controls extending into the sphere of distribution on the other."

A market economy has not one overall plan, but many plans based on "highly developed methods of market research [used] extensively for the systematic recording of economic data and the evaluation of trends." Fighting the trend towards central planning in many postwar economies, he declared: "It is still a widely held fallacy that the outcome of free competition is to arrest movement and change within the social structure or at least to set up economic strains and stresses. In actual fact . . . it is precisely the other way round, . . . it is the limiting of freedom of movement that throws the economy out of balance and produces crisis after crisis, each more unmanageable than the last." This used to be the most telling indictment of capitalist free markets. While capitalist economies in the post-World War II era seem to have overcome the problems of periodic booms

1

and busts, the record of the centrally planned economies (communist and noncommunist) seem to lend some substance to Erhard's charge. The American economist Harry Shaffer, pointing to the slowing of Czech growth between 1957 and 1960, claims that "in 1963 Czechoslovakia became the only industrialized country in the entire world to register a decrease in industrial output, national income, and real wages." (See p. 71 in this volume.)

Erhard is not a laissez-faire economist nor is the West German "miracle" of economic recovery and expansion, of which he is a leading architect, an example of what unrestrained government free enterprise can do. The West German government pursues activist economic policies to counter some and strengthen other market forces. Nonetheless, its main thrust has been toward less rather than more government intervention in the economy.[1] The West German economy has experienced very high rates of growth for almost two decades now, and it is difficult not to credit her economic policies with much of this success.[2]

West German success, however, did not prevent France from adopting policies often described as "indicative planning." The French economy is in essence a free market, private enterprise economy in which the state has traditionally played a large role in the regulation, direction operation and even ownership of enterprises.

The traditions of competition have not been very strong because of the dominance of markets by a few large family enterprises and the prevalence of a social ethic involving concepts like the "just price," the "just wage" and "live and let live."[3] While there are

[1] See Egon Sohmen, "Competition and Growth: The Lesson of West Germany," *American Economic Review,* December 1959, pp. 986–1003 and the discussion, pp. 1003–1031. According to one view, an easy money policy and deliberate undervaluation of the Mark can account for much of Germany's success in generating foreign trade surpluses and high growth rates; see Hans O. Schmidt, "The West German Miracle Reconsidered," *Challenge,* February 1965, pp. 4–6. A similar view ascribes the high growth rates of Western European and Japanese economies to the willingness of the U.S. to run up large balance of payment deficits with these economies, thus providing them with a ready and vast market for their exports; see Richard N. Cooper, "Dollar Deficits and Postwar Economic Growth," *The Review of Economics and Statistics,* XLVI, 2 (May 1964), pp. 155–159.

[2] See eg. Ludwig Erhard, *Prosperity Through Competition,* Praeger, New York, 1958, ch. V, and pp. 81–99, 178–184; for another perspective on this see Karl W. Roskamp, "Lessons from the West German Miracle," *Challenge,* July 1, 1961, pp. 10–14.

some coercive elements in the toolbox used to implement the plans, by and large, the plans are drawn up and carried out through forecasting economic trends, indicating desired and feasible output goals and helping businesses in implementing *their* investment goals provided these are consistent with the national plans. The head of the French Commissariat of Planning, Pierre Massé, outlines this mechanism for obtaining a democratic consensus on the desired and feasible economic goals of the nation and the measures to achieve these goals through the market. A relatively sluggish French economy has in recent years displayed a healthy rate of growth (about 5.5% compared to West Germany's 8%).

The special correspondent of *The Economist* describes some features of Japan's version of indicative planning. Japan's GNP has grown by over 8.5% for almost a decade. This economy, with its unique institutions, cultural traditions, and market structure, and through a rather unconventional monetary and fiscal policy continues to demonstrate perhaps the most dynamic performance of all the industrialized nations.[4]

"Where there is growth there must be initiative somewhere" observes Gregory Grossman. The nature, extent, and purpose of this initiative varies from government to government. In the Soviet Union "the locus of this initiative . . . has been from the start and continues to be the country's political leadership." Professor Grossman examines the resistances to growth and innovation as well as the pressures to overcome these resistances. He points out that these pressures have been routinized and that the danger of stagnation as a result of easing of the pressures from the top is always there. But, he asks, "Are not the inertia and conservatism, which the pressure from above seeks to overcome, themselves results of the center's iron grip on the economy? Should this grip loosen as the pressure diminishes, might not other, more spontaneous and to us more familiar, sources of drive come to the surface? One would think so . . ."[5] Many Russian and

[3] Alfred Oxenfeldt and Vsevolod Holubnychy, *Economic Systems in Action* (New York: Holt, Rinehart and Winston, 3rd ed., 1965), pp. 167–239.

[4] See Shigeto Tsuru, "Growth and Stability of the Postwar Japanese Economy," *The American Economic Review*, Vol. LI, No. 2 (May 1961), pp. 400–411; also, Kazushi Ohkawa, "Recent Japanese Growth in Historical Perspective," *American Economic Review*, May 1963, pp. 578–588.

[5] Gregory Grossman, "Soviet Growth: Routine, Inertia, and Pressure," *American Economic Review* (May 1960), pp. 62–72.

Eastern European economists such as Anton Klas think so too. Professor Klas using the language of cybernetics makes a strong case for the market mechanism.

Western economists have produced the best critiques of the market mechanism and market economies. It is a sign of social and political maturity that centrally planned economies should now be producing the best critiques of centrally planned economies.

LUDWIG ERHARD

Free Economy versus Planned Economy*

Local government elections in the Länder *demonstrated the German people's will to live, to turn away from despair, and to shun both nationalism and communism, and this in spite of the fact that food rations still fell short of 1,500 calories a day per head of the population. All attempts at mending matters were frustrated, not only by the prevailing conditions of devastation, exhaustion and disruption, but also by the supposed experts, in and outside Germany, clinging tenaciously to their reliance on controls. The people worked on doggedly, tormented by hunger and exasperated by zonal restrictions, corruption and the black market. The outlines of a new approach emerge in the following article, the title of which at once indicates the dividing line along which the intellectual and political arguments of those days were ranged.*

IN THE WORK of threshing out the *Länder* constitutions, discussion of what shape the future economic order should take naturally occupied an important place. I shall attempt in this article to disen-

* From Ludwig Erhard, *The Economics of Success,* tr. J. A. Arengo-Jones and D. J. S. Thomson (London, 1963), pp. 7–10. Reprinted by permission of Thames and Hudson Ltd.

tangle the specific problems of the moment from the web of polemics and to make a sober assessment of our position by formulating what is common to all the proposals that have so far emerged. It is typical of our present situation that these conflicting views should invariably be pushed to extremes terminating on opposite sides of a supposedly unbridgeable gulf — on one side free economy, on the other planned economy, here socialism, there capitalism — although the economic developments actually taking place should rather make us ask ourselves whether influences are not in fact emanating from both fronts and tending to bridge the gap between conflicting viewpoints. To imagine, for instance, that any free economy must exhibit symptoms of the uninhibited exploitation associated with the early days of capitalism is to misunderstand the dynamism of the advanced economies of today as completely as does the detached individualist for whom any kind of economic planning is tantamount to the life-destroying levelling of a soulless bureaucracy. And the same applies in regard to the concepts of capitalism and socialism. Today it is just as hopelessly biased to think that capitalism means exploitation of the workers as it is to think that socialism means the ruthless denial of the last trace of freedom. If, for example, the main characteristic of a capitalist economy is taken to be merely the capitalist mode of production involving the large-scale investment of capital formed within the national economy, then there is no difference between it and a socialist economy. Conversely, a free economy, which simply because it is free is commonly dubbed "capitalist," need not preclude full regard for the social needs of the day. And whereas in capitalist countries with a free market economy the accumulation of capital is often violently criticized, the formation and use of capital in socialist countries is often not subjected to such effective public scrutiny and criticism. In other words, catch-phrase criteria are no longer applicable in appraising an economic system, least of all its social aspects. When it is remembered that a capitalist and a socialist economy are equally compelled to make provision for the building up of capital resources, and at the same time it is agreed that this can only be done, whatever the shape of the economic structure may be, by saving and consumer restraint, then it looks very much as if the systems are not so irreconcilable after all.

It is indeed true that a socialist economy cannot do without planning on an extensive scale, but this does not mean that a free economy — or, to be more precise, a market economy — can be written off as aimless or anarchical. The fact is that it uses the highly developed methods of market research so extensively for the systematic recording of economic data and the evaluation of trends, that with this type of economic order there is a very strong and growing tendency to put plans first. In an earlier article I pointed out that between an economy which embraces many plans and a fully planned economy there are any number of possible systems, varying according to the particular kind or degree of influence or guidance brought to bear on the functions of the economy, and that it is therefore wrong and dishonest in this connection to play around with absolutes.

The real contradistinction is not between free and planned economic systems, nor between capitalist and socialist economic systems, but between a market economy with free price-level adjustment on the one hand and an authoritarian economy with state controls extending into the sphere of distribution on the other. In the last analysis it is simply a question of whether the market as the voice of the economic society as a whole or, alternatively, the state or some other collective entity is better able to decide what is conducive to the common good or the well-being of all. It is still a widely held fallacy that the outcome of free competition is to arrest movement and change within the social structure or at least to set up economic strains and stresses. In actual fact, all liberal-minded experts with a sound knowledge of the social organisms are agreed that it is precisely the other way round, that it is the limiting of freedom of movement that throws the economy out of balance and produces crisis after crisis, each more unmanageable than the last. Provided in future the state sees to it that neither social privileges nor artificial monopolies impede the natural process by which economic forces reach and maintain a state of equilibrium, and that the operation of supply and demand is allowed free play, the market will adjust the total input of economic forces so as to create optimum running conditions and to compensate any mistakes made at the controls. Anyone who wishes is welcome to believe that a planning and regulating economic authority might be a better judge of the economic intentions and wishes of society; but just let him try to prove it. What can be said is that in a free market economy mistakes of judgment in the management of affairs automatically produce price changes with all their attendant repercussions, whereas in a state-directed economy there is always the danger that equally serious mistakes can be covered up and left to fester until they ultimately erupt with elemental force. We have had experience in recent years of how easily a state-directed economy can deteriorate, by imperceptible stages, into a travesty of what an economy should be.

Our criticism is thus not directed against the planned economy *per se,* whose manifold forms can be variously interpreted, but most definitely against the state-controlled authoritarian economy, which if carried to its logical conclusion wipes out the market and robs the consumer of all freedom of choice. On the other hand, a collectively managed economy responsive to market reactions is a contradiction in terms and therefore unthinkable; disregard for the wishes of the consumer as reflected in market reactions is bound to destroy freedom of action and stems from the fallacy that human happiness can be secured by maximum satisfaction of statistically measurable needs. So, even assuming that the authority wielding economic control had no other motive than to serve the good of the community — and this not even the socialist state guarantees — it is still open to doubt whether the people as a whole would prefer any form of collective economy to the free market economy.

As things are today, the state must provide the economy with the principles and broad lines of a policy and with objectives designed to guide and regulate its functioning. In this respect the state indisputably has and should have the initiative. But to go further and reduce the independent businessman to the status of a mere puppet or servant of the authority's will would be to destroy all the values derived from personality and to rob the economy of its most precious source of inspiration and strength. Now, if ever, is the time to realize that the economy is not opposed to social progress but, on the contrary, treats it as a yardstick. All steps capable of contributing to a fair distribution of the national product, and with it of the national income, deserve our most careful consideration. But then we have the chance to do this through the very act of honouring the obligations arising from our country's distress, if only we put actuality before dogma.

I am convinced that the tasks of today call for the full participation of the individual. We shall be doing our country a real and lasting service if we establish an economic order which is purged of the theorizing and bureaucratic spirit that everyone hates and which enables people to act freely in response to a sense of their social responsibilities.

PIERRE MASSÉ

The Economic Planning
Experience of France*

DEVELOPMENT plans for the French economy are the main products of my organization, the Commissariat Général du Plan, which is a branch of the Prime Minister's office, the equivalent of what would be called here an Agency in the Executive branch of the Federal Government. I think I should first try to give you an idea of what such a development plan actually is.

Physically, it is a book, about 250 pages long. The first page contains the text of a law, signed by the President and Ministers. It says something like "The development plan published as an annex to this law is approved as a guide for the economy to follow and as a framework for all investment programs."

The remaining 249 pages contain the "approved" plan: not a law in itself, but a document approbated by a law. It usually covers a forthcoming period of four years. It begins with a general assessment of the problems and potentialities of the French economy and of its past achievements, from which are drawn the main lines of development for the period covered: rate of growth of national production; level of employment in agriculture, industry, and other sectors; rate of capital formation; estimates of exports and imports. Then come the statements of government policy intentions: amount of military expenditures, foreign aid, and scientific research; allocation of the bulk of resources which remain in the economy among private disposable income, non-wage benefits, and investments for projects of public interest (schools, hospitals, city planning, etc.); the fiscal provisions, incentives, and other means by which the state will help the economy reach the goals set.

After this general outline comes a section which deals with the requirements to be met in order to achieve these national objectives: training and allocation of manpower, technological research, balance

* From Pierre Massé, "The Economic Planning Experience of France," *Looking Ahead* (January 1963), pp. 1–14. Reprinted by permission of *Looking Ahead* and of the National Planning Association.

of foreign trade and payments, savings toward investment, tax structure, countercyclical provisions, and many other requirements. Finally comes the thickest part of the book: comparatively detailed chapters describing the contemplated growth process for each sector of the economy, and of the economic or social activities of the government.

I believe it is interesting that these planned targets are listed together with reference to a single period of time, and all checked against one another, so as to be mutually consistent.

Any large firm operated on modern lines draws up medium- and long-term programs, in which market forecasts, new equipment expenditures, and all aspects of the firm's policy are made mutually consistent in order to adjust the objectives to the means available to achieve them, and vice versa. The steel producer makes sure of his supplies of ore and coke, evaluates his markets in the metal-working and construction industries, keeps informed of his competitors' plans. He makes his decisions only after a detailed survey of his industrial environment. But, in limiting himself to this environment, he may overlook fields of activity which appear far removed from his own and which are, nevertheless, capable of influencing his position. Changes in agricultural income, for example, react progressively throughout the economy and, after affecting the production of tractors, finally influence sales of steel.

The idea behind the plan is to integrate all these phenomena of interdependence within the scope of a multisector study; to program economic activities in general terms, so that any branch may buy its supplies and sell its products on balanced markets.

THE METHOD OF PLANNING

Let us now review very briefly a few points of method. I would like to begin with a rough sketch of the planning procedure we use, at least in its present state.

The first phase of preparation of a plan is the drawing up of alternative schemes of development, so as to explore the future possibilities of the economy, and to come to a decision about the best general course to follow during the plan period, accompanied by a hypothesis concerning foreign trade and another concerning the level of investment required to carry on expansion along this period. From such data, conventional input-output techniques allow us to set up for the last year of the period an economic table, in which the economy is broken down into 28 sectors.

In principle, one may say that the best scheme is the one which considers the maximum growth rate of the economy, while taking into account basic equilibriums: full employment, investment equal to savings, balance of public finance and of foreign payments.

The choice which is made by the Cabinet upon my proposals, and after due consultations, is made not only in terms of the rate of growth, but also takes into account the basic features of the distribution of the new resources created by expansion.

Once the Cabinet has approved a general scheme, which amounts simultaneously to a statement of policy intentions and to a coherent framework in which to fit the detailed programs of each sector, those detailed programs are prepared by the planning committee; this is what I call the second phase of the preparation, where those responsible for the actual daily functioning of the economy take over, after the economists and the general policy makers have completed their task.

In the course of this second phase, basic alterations can be made in the initial scheme, if the experience of the committee members suggests a correction to the calculations of the economists; and this is where our "general market survey," as I described it earlier, is carried out.

My duty during this second phase is to make sure that the various targets proposed by the committees remain consistent, and to prepare a final summary for presentation to the Government and the Parliament.

PLANNING BY THE PLANNED

The method of planning has nothing to do with a detailed, bureaucratic control of the economy. Why?

First, because the program is worked out in terms of branches of activity and not of companies or products. It respects and assists free enterprise. Secondly, because it is drawn up with the cooperation of all the nation's political, economic, and social forces. Lastly, because in practice economic means are preferred, for reasons of principle, to administrative measures.

I shall deal with these three points in turn:

The plan is established by each branch of activity. It does not dictate a course of action to private enterprise. It simply states the general objectives set for economic development and the particular goal for each branch. But, within the framework thus outlined, each firm is free to choose its own target. It can maintain its share within its branch, it can increase it, it can reduce it — that is its own affair.

It acts on the basis of better information, but at its own risk. But, in return, the plan lets the firm assume its own responsibilities.

Furthermore, there is in general no noticeable discrepancy between the target of the branch and the sum of the targets of individual companies, because of the concerted planning procedure which I am now going to describe.

The plan seeks to combine all the political, economic, and social forces of the nation. In the First Plan, Mr. Jean Monnet was already using the expression "concerted economy" which has recently gained popularity.

Useful as it may be, I do not think our national "market survey" would be a great success if it were made by a specialized group of bureaucrats for the people who make the daily decisions. The whole philosophy of our methods is to have the plan made by those who will have to follow it, not for them or against them.

The most specific task of my office is to organize and coordinate the work of 25 planning committees appointed by the Government for the detailed preparation of each four-year plan. Twenty of them deal with a sector of production or a branch of the public services: agriculture, transportation, chemicals, schools and universities, urban renewal, and so on. They thus cover every field where any investment takes place. The remaining five committees deal with general problems: manpower, over-all balance and financing, research, productivity, regional planning. Each committee includes, as a rule, officials from the ministries concerned, personally appointed heads of firms (when the committee deals with an industry), representatives of business associations and of labor unions, and individual experts.

The committees usually divide themselves into a number of working parties, each of which covers either a fraction of the committee's sector, or one of the aspects of the plan for the whole sector. Such parties must include members of the same broad categories as the committees do. Usually a few of them come from the committee itself. The total force thus mobilized in the process of detailed planning is of about 3,500 persons, a good sampling of the influential circles in the French economy.

In fact, the best description of our work is: "Planning without Planners," or "Planning by the Planned." This procedure is slow and imperfect. It leads to unsatisfactory compromises, and it consumes a lot of energy. But I think it is the only sort of planning procedure suitable for an economy of free enterprise.

And, of course, the feeling of participation created by such a procedure is quite gratifying for each individual involved, and really creates a spirit of common purpose throughout the whole economic system as well as in government and political circles.

The French Plan is not compulsory. Nevertheless, it is put into practice. For the last three years in particular it has been put into practice most efficiently, with a few deviations which are insignificant in relation to the target of expansion.

This is no miracle, it is simply that a number of positive factors have worked together toward a common goal in a way which is interesting to examine.

As has already been said, all those who will be responsible for implementing the plan have had a hand, directly or indirectly, in its formulation. Moreover, if everybody plays the game, the plan ensures that each branch of production is matched by solvent demand.

Through investments made by all its agencies and by the nationalized industries, to which must be added state-subsidized housing, the government supervises half of the total investments. And these investments themselves act as a spur on the adjacent sectors (for example, French National Power Company and French National Railways on the electrical manufacturing industry).

The state can influence the private sector by economic means and administrative measures. It systematically prefers to employ economic means, or stimulants, namely by granting loans, tax exemptions, or subsidies for projects which are consistent with the plan.

It must be added that these various factors do not constitute an absolute guarantee that the plan will be carried to a successful conclusion in a rapidly changing world.

If unforeseen circumstances jeopardize implementation of the plan, the government first attempts to maintain the targets by suitably adapting the means employed. However, the situation can become such that it would be foolish to seek to maintain the targets at any price. In such a case, the plan is adjusted or revised; this happened toward the middle of the Third Plan and an interim plan was formulated, which fixed as a target an average rate of expansion of 5.5 percent for the years 1960 and 1961.

THE PLAN'S ROLE IN POSTWAR EXPANSION

What has been the role of the Plan in French postwar expansion? This is a much debated question to which I should like to give an objective reply.

French expansion has been achieved during the past sixteen years with a constant labor force, which has not been the case in either

Italy or Germany. The credit is due above all to the French people, to their work, their ingenuity, and the rejuvenation of the population. French expansion has been, to use Toynbee's expression, their reply to a challenge, the challenge of defeat and enemy occupation.

A second factor contributing to this success was the creation of the European Economic Community, which has provided French agriculture and industry with new outlets, but has at the same time exposed them to stimulating competition. However, these different factors must not obscure the role played by the Plan.

The Plan has contributed to a better understanding of the realities of the economic situation. Moreover, it has encouraged industries to adopt within a coherent total environment higher targets than they would have chosen spontaneously. I could quote specific examples in support of this opinion (electricity, steel).

On the other hand, it must be said that although the Plan has contributed to expansion, it has not in the past succeeded in avoiding inflation. The financial recovery of 1959 is fundamentally due to other causes: political stability, devaluation carried out with technical efficiency, the influence of trade liberalization, and the emergence of the Common Market. But it must be added that these favorable factors found support in the large-scale investments already made with the help of the Plan. Furthermore, since 1959, the Plan has in turn found its support in a stabilized financial situation, and has contributed to the achievement of a balanced expansion at the rather remarkable average annual rate of 5.5 percent during the three years 1960, 1961, and 1962. The French Government has also recently begun working toward a definition of an income policy within the framework of the Plan. This policy strives to reconcile social justice with the intent to avoid the return of inflation, which would jeopardize the continuity of expansion. The economic maturity of the French free labor unions has made this endeavor possible, and will also, I hope, further its progress.

NEW PROBLEMS FOR PLANNERS

French planning, which I have attempted to describe to you, determined in its objectives and flexible in its methods, finds itself today faced with new problems.

For planning becomes more difficult and hazardous in a country with open frontiers than in one with closed frontiers. Making things easy for the planner cannot be an end in itself, and not for a second can there be any question of not going ahead with the creation of large-scale economic communities for that reason. But it is not impossible to reconcile all factors. The Treaty of Rome, instituting the Common Market, provides for a common agricultural policy. And what is a common agricultural policy other than a draft plan, in the French understanding of the term? The European Economic Community has just submitted to the six governments a memorandum in which the idea of a minimum of concerted programing is set forth.

This memorandum is still under study by the Government and I must therefore be very circumspect in making comments. I can nevertheless say that French planning is sufficiently flexible to lend itself to the adjustments entailed by European cooperation. A general feeling exists in France, however, that it should remain open and democratic in character, with a reasonable priority of targets over means, and should use methods of implementation based on persuasion and stimulation, which in no way curtail the basic human freedoms, including the right to practice free enterprise.

THE ECONOMIST

Consider Japan

The Most Exciting Example

In the decade since [1951] Japan . . . has seen its real national product increase at an average pace of over 9 per cent a year, its industrial production and rate of manufacturing exports more than quadruple, its urban population make the great breakthrough into the first modern consumer-oriented economy in Asia. In the process it has seen the average Japanese's expectation of life (now just over 65 for a man, just over 70 for a woman) rise to ages that are now actually ten years longer than they were only twelve years ago. There are some who will regard this last achievement alone as one of the most exciting and extraordinary sudden forward leaps in the entire economic history of the world.

* From "Consider Japan — I," *The Economist* (September 1962), pp. 793, 795–812. Reprinted by permission of *The Economist*.

. . . Japan possesses one conventional economic "advantage" which explains why it should indeed be able to expect a faster rate of growth than would easily be possible in present-day Britain. This "advantage" is that Japan is still only part of the way forward to being a wealthy and fully developed industrial economy as yet. . . . The workers of Japan — whose *per capita* national income in 1961 still averaged only about two-fifths of Britain's — can fairly reasonably be divided into three broad groups.

Perhaps more than a tenth of the total labour force of 45 million (about 27 million men, 18 million women) work in factories, and other productive establishments that are as efficient as any of their kind in the world, and they are beginning to enjoy a standard of living which is therefore broadly (even if not yet quite) in line with that level of productivity, at any rate when the extensive fringe benefits offered by all the big Japanese firms are included. To this upper tenth will belong perhaps the upper one-fifth of Japan's 21 million "regular workers" in non-agricultural industries.

Perhaps over another quarter of the 45 million work at jobs where their productivity and living standards, although below those in the most modern sector, are still definitely of western rather than Asian status. After all, we are talking here of a country where more than 45 per cent of households (over 60 per cent in the towns, over 25 per cent in the countryside) now possess a television set and where over 17 per cent of urban households possess a refrigerator.

WAGE AND PRODUCTIVITY INDICES BY SIZE OF PLANT

	Japan (1958)		Britain (1949)	
(Over 1,000 workers = 100)				
Number of Workers	Added Value per Worker	Wage per Worker	Added Value per Worker	Wage per Worker
4— 9	27.0	37.9	. . . .	. . . .
10— 50	36.4	43.9	91.4	82.5
50— 99	47.9	50.4	93.8	83.7
100— 499	64.6	61.2	96.4	85.5
500— 999	76.8	75.2	98.1	89.3
Over 1,000	100.0	100.0	100.0	100.0

NOTE — The figures for Britain are worked out from the manufacturing census of 1949, but relativities between big and small firms are unlikely to have changed much in the meantime. Figures for Japan refer to 1958. In the last few years wages — and particularly starting wages for scarce teenage workers — have risen even more quickly in Japan's small firms than in its big ones, but the gap between total productivity of all workers in big and small firms has plainly remained.

But all this must still leave more than half of Japan's 45 million workers in jobs where their level of productivity (and thus of earnings per hour) is less than half of that in the great modern combines. This depressed half must include the majority (though not nowadays all, see feature on "Living Standards" on a later page) of Japan's huge army of 22 million small scale self-employed men and "unpaid family workers." Most of these "family workers" are the country's 15 million farmers and fishermen, and its 1½ million small shopkeepers and petty traders; but other family workers will sweat their whole lives out in Japan's 400,000 "very small" (under 10 workers each) industrial "workshops" which really consist of two or three lathes set up

ECONOMIC GROWTH
(Gross National Product in Real Terms)

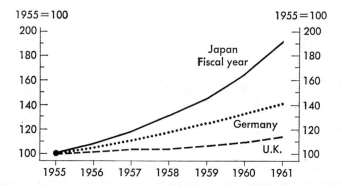

in some family's living room. The depressed half of the labour force will also include Japan's most miserable employed industrial class of a million or so ageing day labourers (average cash earnings in 1961, about 12s. a day); and many even of the regular workers in Japan's mass of small but genuine industrial establishments with between 30 and 100 workers each, in which labour productivity per workers — in sharp contradistinction to Britain (see table on the preceding page and footnote) — is still generally less than half of that in the big factories with 1,000 workers or more.

The scope for expansion in an economy of this sort is therefore very large, merely by switching workers from the wildly unproductive sectors into the much more productive ones. The problem is notably different in degree from that in Britain. But it is not entirely different in kind. Even in Britain, as figures now published regularly by the

Ministry of Labour make clear, average male workers' earnings in new and modern British industries (ranging from motor car manufacture through machine tools and most other forms of engineering to such things as detergents and synthetic resins) are regularly between 20 and 35 per cent higher than those in older sounding industries like textiles (other than the new man-made fibres) of leather goods or footwear or brushes and brooms. These differences are by no means wholly due to differences in innate levels of skills. One of the advantages for a westerner of studying an economy like Japan's is that it makes it abundantly clear how far modern economic progress depends on switching workers out of the second sort of job into the first.

It also suggests that the pace at which the advance can be effected depends mainly on the answers that can be given to three questions:

(1) Whether the modern sector of industry has an incentive and a mood, and is backed by the kind of government economic policy, that encourage it to play an ever bigger and more expansive part in the national economic life;

(2) Whether the purposeful expansion of marginal domestic demand — which is the only means by which these modern sectors of industry can be spurred on to grow — is then liable to run the country into intermittent balance of payments crises; and if so whether the government can find ways of countering those crises without cutting domestic demand back too grievously and for too long;

(3) Whether the social and economic mechanism for encouraging switches of labour and other resources out of the old-fashioned sector into the modern sector works smoothly and well.

The answers to these questions in Japan are that the Japanese government, either by good fortune or good management, has so far solved the first two problems — that of providing incentives for efficient growth industries to grow, and that of riding past its successive balance of payments crises (in 1953–54, 1957 and 1961) without losing its dynamic of growth — with more brilliant success than in any other country in the world.

The answer to the third question is that Japan's social structure and habits could not have been more appallingly devised to make a switch of resources out of the least productive sectors of the economy into the big growth industries more difficult. This is because of the system of lifetime employment and "no new regular jobs for old men" (old meaning anybody over 35) described in a feature on the previous page. This strange employment system explains why Japanese industrialists genuinely claim that they too have been operating in conditions of labour shortage and "over-the-brim-full employment." It makes Japan's achievements in securing an average of over 9 per cent of expansion each year all the more remarkable — and its method of running its economy to achieve this all the more worth studying in the west. It is to these positive lessons of Japan's economic experiment that the next article will turn.

Easy Budgets . . .

Japan's system of managing its economy has been to run what would be regarded in Britain as very expansionary budget policies, with large planned increases in government expenditure and sizeable reductions in personal taxation a regular feature of most recent years (see following table); and to use monetary policy and rises in interest rates as the main restraining weapons, when and if any restraints are needed. This pattern has been widely misunderstood abroad, because of the barriers which economists (particularly government economists) raise in the way of understanding each others' language.

Most Japanese economists will worthily insist — and American economic commentators will generally approvingly report — that Japan has constantly balanced its annual estimates of budget expenditure and revenue ever since Mr. Dodge laid down that balanced budget estimates were the right thing to have. But the balancing act is done in a very peculiar way.

Around the turn of every calendar year (and thus three or four months before the fiscal year begins on April 1st) everybody in Japan seems to enter into an annual guessing game to recommend what the target rate for growth in next year's gross national product should be. The ruling Liberal Democratic party, in solemn convention assembled, recommends that gross national product should grow at one rate; the Ministry of Finance recommends that it would be safer to aim to grow at a slightly lower rate; the Economic Planning Agency makes a final calculation, and the Cabinet splits the differences. Thus one reads in the newspapers that the Cabinet after a long session decided that the rate of growth should be 9.2 per cent in fiscal 1961 or 5.4 per cent in fiscal 1962.

This apparently absurd guessing game, expressed to a precise point of decimals, has a genuine economic importance. For every 0.1 per cent of the agreed target rate for growth in national income the Japanese reckon that they can expect a stated amount of extra tax revenue on the basis of existing tax rates. Thus with a target growth rate of 5.4 per cent this fiscal year, they reckoned on nearly £500 million of extra revenue; and by the rules of the budget balancing act precisely that sum — together with the surplus of tax revenue carried over from the previous year — is then assumed to be available for deliberate increases in government expenditure or for new tax reliefs. The remarkable feature of the game, from the reflationist's point of view, is that the larger the target figure for growth which the planners-cum-bargainers eventually decide upon — and the bigger the growth in production in the preceding year (i.e., the nearer the economy has been running to capacity) — the bigger the tax reliefs and deliberate

JAPAN'S DECADE OF TAX RELIEFS

		Value of Tax Relief in That Year's Budget		
Fiscal Year	Current Balance of Payments Deficit (−) or Surplus (+)*	On Personal Income Tax	On All Taxes	Growth in Real GNP %
1951	+118	61	113	+13.5
1952	+112	113	90	+10.5
1953	− 69	77	124	+ 6.7
1954	+ 36	31	17	+ 3.9
1955	+177	53	66	+10.1
1956	+104	23	2	+ 8.2
1957	−137	110	62	+ 7.1
1958	+183	6	37	+ 3.7
1959	+121	23	10	+17.7
1960	+ 39	Nil	− 7	+13.2
1961	−388	56	75	+15.2*
1962		47	116	

Caption: (Billions of Yen, which virtually equal millions of pounds)

* Calendar year.

increases in government expenditure which this system tells them it is orthodox for them to give away.

These reliefs, be it noted, are regarded as "orthodox" even in years when the balance of payments has run into large deficit. Indeed, if the gross national product has been rising particularly swiftly during a year of balance-of-payments crisis — which will usually be the case since Japanese balance of payments troubles are generally of the import *boomu* (Japanese-English for boom) type — it is practically certain that the uncovenanted surplus of tax revenue to be carried over into the next year, and probable that the rise in national income to be counted on for the next year as a whole, will be correspondingly high also. Under the rules of the game, this makes it "orthodox" to make the new year's tax relief or deliberate increase in government expenditure particularly large. Thus in the middle of the balance of payments crisis of 1957 (while Japan's international exchange reserves were dropping sharply) the income tax levied on the average lower middle class and upper working class salary was literally cut in half. During this last year's balance of payments crisis, Japanese taxes were reduced by about £116 million (at a time when Mr. Selwyn Lloyd, in his July and April budgets combined, was raising British taxes by over £200 million); and this Japanese cut of £116 million, reported the *Oriental Economist* truthfully, aroused "general public complaint of a conservative tax relief."

In this circumstances it may seem a bit odd that the Japanese economy ever slows down at all, at any point short of raging inflation. But — at least until this last year, when living costs in the cities have suddenly bounded by 10 per cent — the policy has not in fact proved very inflationary (the urban consumer price index rose by some 20 per cent in Japan between 1953 and 1961, against a rise of just over 25 per cent in Britain, while Japan's export price index has actually fallen in this period). Moreover — again until last year — Japan has managed to escape out of its balance of payments crises and periods of "overheating," back on to expansion again, much more quickly than Britain. The weapon used to counter periods of overheating has never been fiscal, but always monetary, policy.

The way in which a restrictive monetary policy is worked in Japan at times of balance of payments difficulty — once again, to the foreigner it seems a very peculiar way — will be discussed in the next article. But it is worth pausing here to consider the rationale of their system. It is customary in Britain to say that monetary policy cannot work as a restrictive device in times of balance of payments crisis if budgetary policy is pulling the opposite way. Experience in Japan goes a long way towards casting doubt on this belief — because their experience is that the two weapons work with quite different time intervals of effectiveness. Monetary policy works much the more quickly and much the more directly upon the balance of payments, both on capital account (by drawing in loanable funds, such as Euro-dollars, from abroad) and on current account (by cutting down imports). By contrast, restriction of demand by higher tax rates works on the balance of payments only after a time lag; and the Japanese say that at times of balance of payments trouble the restriction of demand and imports after a time lag is likely to be the precise reverse of what they want.

Japan's main imports are (like Britain's) raw materials and (less like Britain's) machinery. Both of these forms of imports tend to be highly cyclical (the Japanese recognise, which the British do not always do, that a rush of imports during the period of restocking or investment boom is likely to be followed by a period of natural slowing down on the reverse arm of the cycle); and both are bought almost wholly on business account. The Japanese reckon that a change in interest rates can alter business spending very quickly. No doubt this swift effect is partly due to the peculiar capital composition of Japanese business enterprises (whose loan capital, on which interest has to be paid, constitutes about 70 per cent of aggregate capital). But one suspects that even in countries like Britain a sharp rise in Bank rate can begin to affect businesses' inventory policies within a fairly short period, while changes in tax rates work much more slowly than Bank rate, at least as a restraining device; when Mr. Selwyn Lloyd increases the fuel oil tax, for example, there may be some small initial effect on total spending, but a main effect will be to reduce the number of people who would otherwise be using oil for energy purposes anything from six months to three years hence.

Most British policy-makers would presumably agree that usually they do not really know what they will want demand to be doing more than six months or so ahead. The best Japanese planners, by contrast, will say that they do know what they want demand to be doing in the long term; they want it, and production, to be rising by 7 or 8 per cent a year (or whatever is the figure consistent with furtherance of their current long-term plan). It therefore seems logical to them to use fiscal policy as an instrument for steadily increasing long-term demand by something approaching the long-term target figure, while using monetary policy as the weapon to control cyclical fluctuations in the balance of payments during that forward march.

Because the system on which the Japanese budget is drawn up seems so very peculiar — because it appears to encourage inflationary budgets when inflation is already in progress, and could theoretically signal that Japan should introduce a deflationary budget when a recession has cut down tax receipts — it takes some time for the visitor to Tokyo to recognise that the Japanese method of organising economic policy is as sophisticated as it is. But by the end of his stay your correspondent was convinced that the degree of sophistication on these matters in Japan — albeit often behind a screen of flummery words designed to show that they were all very simple and conventional chaps with a lot to learn from the West — is really very high indeed. It also happens to have been a sophistication that works.

. . . But Tight Money

The monetary policy of the Bank of Japan provides a fascinating study for the visiting foreign economist, like almost everything else in this land. It is very difficult to decide whether the policy's undoubted effectiveness has been the result of the Bank's extraordinary success in making the brilliant best of a bad job, or whether the bad job itself (as represented by the highly unorthodox nature of the Japanese commercial banking system) has paradoxically made monetary control very much easier. For various historical reasons (of which the failure of the cheque system to develop quickly under Japanese conditions is one) commercial banking business in Japan is profitable only if the big city banks operate at levels of illiquidity that would drive an English or American banker into a state of permanent neurosis. When window dressing (which is considerable) is removed, the city banks' real cash ratio against deposits is only about 2 or 3 per cent, and they hold virtually no other genuinely liquid assets at all (compare the British commercial banks' conventional liquidity ratio of 30 per cent). The other 97 or 98 per cent of their deposited money is out on loan, without many of the usual conventional bankers' distinctions about lending only for short term requirements; a very large part of Japan's massive investment boom in fixed capital equipment has been financed by commercial bank loans.

The result of this "overloan position" is that the city banks periodically find themselves in a desperate need to raise liquid funds from somewhere, either in order to meet emergencies or else simply in order to increase their lending further. They can do this in two ways. They can borrow some emergency funds from each other (or from rural and other savings institutions) on the so-called call loan market, interest rates on which can sometimes reach fantastic heights; at one stage during the last balance of payments crisis and credit squeeze call money was being borrowed by the big city banks at over 20 per cent. The other source, nominally as a lender of last resort but really as the main engine of capital creation during a boom, is the Bank of Japan. The Bank's process of credit creation went forward particularly heavily during the early years of Japanese recovery, so that Japanese bankers themselves admitted — and visiting American bankers reported back with horror — that "the commercial banks in the early nineteen-fifties became merely a channel through which the central bank fed industry with investment funds." It was this "overloan" position that Mr. Dodge referred to with indignation when he castigated (as mentioned in our first article) the illusion "that granting progressively larger amounts of commercial bank credit for capital purposes can be substituted for the normal process of capital accumulation."

Nevertheless the fact remains that it was substituted, and that it has worked. Looking round the shining new factories of Japan — a country that actually had the greater part of its previous industrial capacity destroyed in the war of only seventeen years ago — nobody can doubt that. Moreover, paradoxical though this may seem, the consequence of the central bank's unorthodoxy during this period has been its rebirth as one of the most powerful central banking organisations in the world. Because the commercial bankers have to come begging to it when they want new funds to increase their lending further, the entire credit structure of Japan now seems to the visiting foreigner to lie snugly under the Bank of Japan's control.

The Bank itself would deny this; its position of absolute power, as lender of last resort, over the credit situation does sometimes mean that it cannot use that power to quite the extent that its exasperation with some aspects of the *boomu* might make it wish to do. It cannot very well turn away big banks who ask it for funds if the result would be to cause a massive financial crash of Overend Gurney proportions. But in banking, as in international diplomacy, an authority that possesses an unusable thermonuclear deterrent does not necessarily thereby become less able than an unarmed country to make its wishes felt.

The control by the Bank of Japan is exercised in various ways. The one "orthodox" weapon is Bank rate, this summer at 7.3 per cent, which it is certainly able to make effective; most of Japan's other (very high) interest rates are tied to it, and Japanese businesses' heavy dependence on borrowing means that they are very susceptible to changes in borrowing rates. A second and more controversial weapon is the so-called "window operation." The Bank of Japan holds regular consultations with the commercial banks, reviews the likely trend of advances of each bank for perhaps a month ahead, and warns individual banks (or, at times of balance of payments crises, warns all big city banks) that they should please start to restrain their advances; if necessary it will even suggest an "overall loan level" for the big banks as a whole. Finally, although the Bank will not generally in the last resort refuse to lend to any big bank, it does levy penalty rates on what it regards as its ultimate margin of less desirable loans to the commercial banks. As part of the same process the Bank of Japan will offer favourable discount rates on particular types of lending paper — especially, to the annoyance of competing British exporters, it will help indirectly to subsidise Japanese exports in this way.

The commercial banks in turn also have a schedule of penalty rates which they levy on those who borrow from them, according to the status of the borrower concerned. And when they have to cut back lending, they have no hesitation about putting pressure on borrowers whose position they regard as unsound. The small local banks, who lend mostly to smaller local firms, will do the same thing when a credit squeeze makes it more profitable for them to use some of their funds in other ways (perhaps, for example, to lend call money to the big city banks at very high interest rates). The consequence is that tight money during credit squeezes can lead to bankruptcies of small firms in Japan. The figures for dishonoured bills (52,470 in January) are one economic indicator that is regularly watched. So is the number of bankruptcies (firms with debts exceeding £10,000) – which was 202 in January, close to the last peak of July, 1957. But at the same time as reporting this, the Japanese press also reported that the Government seemed to be more intent than in previous crises to temper the wind to the smaller shorn lambs.

The more closely one studies the history of the Japanese economy in the last decade, the more one become convinced that success in economic policy nowadays springs from a policy of favouring the forward-looking and most prospering and efficient firms, and beating the less efficient ones into the ground. The fact that control through monetary policy in Japan has – until this last year – generally worked in this direction may not be a sign of great social and humanitarian virtue . . . but it has been of enormous economic utility. Your correspondent became convinced that there are two important lessons for Britain here.

First, the general British method, during the crises of the last decade, of restraining demand by tough budgets and tax regulators has automatically laid its main restraining power on the growth industries, while the opposite Japanese method has worked the other way round. Growth industries, by definition, are those that will be given the bigger impetus to expand their production when the next few hundred million pounds' worth of marginal demand is pumped into the economy; so, of course, they are also those that suffer most severely when the next few hundred million pounds' worth of marginal demand is siphoned out of the economy by means of a restrictive budget. By contrast, the Japanese method of pumping in extra demand through stimulatory budgets, and then using monetary policy and high interest rates as a rationing device, has caused restriction to impinge mainly on those whom the banks regard as the worst business risks. The rationed capital has become available only to those who can use it most profitably — except when political considerations intervene and gum the process up.

Secondly, the British have got used to saying that a policy of expansionary budgets and high interest rates will penalise investment at the expense of stimulating consumption. Japanese experience surely proves this to be nonsense. Japan (where industrial borrowing in recent years has cost about 10 per cent) has recently been devoting nearly 40 per cent of its gross national product to total investment. Britain, on the same basis of comparison, has devoted less than 20 per cent. The truth is that it is a spirit of dynamism among thrusting

RATIO OF INVESTMENT TO GROSS NATIONAL PRODUCT
(1960 figures)

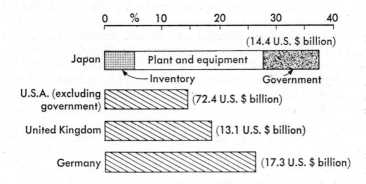

growth industries that nowadays serves to impel an economy along the high road of expanding investment. A policy of stimulatory budgets provides the oats that beckon the horse forward, while a policy of high interest rates provides the reins to guide the horse and also (at least in Japan) helps to provide the high savings (and, sometimes, at appropriate moments of the trade cycle, also the temporary increase of borrowing from abroad) which make the continuance of heavy investment possible. A policy of low interest rates relaxes the reins so that the horse will find it easier to rush forward faster if it wishes, but this is not much use when, because of a lack of expansion of marginal demand, the horse itself is standing still.

The Planning of Exports

It would be absurd to pretend that the success of Japanese governments' economic policies has been due to the formula explained in
the last two articles — easy budgets, but tight money — alone. But
that almost accidental formula has provided the right elbow room
for a part of Japan's dynamic that really has been fundamental;
namely, the nation's economic tendency to look constantly ahead in
emulation.

In part, of course, this springs from Japan's advantage in not
having been historically the front runner in the technological race;
in part, it springs from the very useful national urge to be always
gaining face. If "advanced countries" abroad have a competitive
petrochemical industry — and Japan has not — then everybody in the
Japanese government, and everybody in each big business group
around each of the big banks, wants Japan (and for that matter his
own banking group) to have a successful petrochemical industry too.
Every big firm has a planning division which assiduously studies the
filing of new patents and the introduction of new industrial techniques abroad; when successful ones appear, Japanese industrialists
will immediately enter into negotiations to be allowed to operate the
same techniques, under licence — and nowadays often with considerable locally-added improvements — in Japan. This technological élan
seems to be far more energetic than in British industry, which has
too often seemed to regard the "copying" under licence of American
or other foreign techniques as rather infra dig.

The same tendency for the Japanese to be constantly looking
ahead in emulation permeates their government machine. The Japanese will always tell you, especially if they assume you to be an
American, that theirs is not a planned economy. In the socialist sense
of the term it is not. But Japan, even more than France, is the land
of indicative economic planning à outrance. One has only to read
the annual economic survey published by its Economic Planning
Agency — a colossal tome of 500 magazine-size pages — to appreciate
that. One has also only to look into the economics and statistics
departments of any of its government departments or agencies: huge
factory-like rooms, with economic graduates sitting row upon row, all
hammering out on their adding machines the indicative economic
statistics of the new Japan. Sometimes this estimating goes to what,
to a Briton, seems more than slightly comical extremes: it is a bit odd
to read in the press that the Economic Planning Agency has set a
"target figure" for a rise of 2.8 per cent in the cost of living, or 14.6

per cent in exports, for the year ahead. But the attitude engendered by all this is important, because it is often precisely the opposite of that which rules in Britain. Nowhere can this be seen more startlingly than in Japan's mode of planning its exports, a field in which the Japanese will at first tell one most insistently that they do not do any positive planning at all.

Japan knows exactly where it wants to go in its future export drive. It wants to go into what it calls "heavy and chemical industries' products (totals of machinery, metals, metal products and chemical goods)" — hereafter called heavy goods for short. In 1953, when Japan started its present export advance, it had 50.2 per cent of its exports in light industrial goods (of which three-quarters were textiles) and 35.7 per cent in heavy goods; by 1959 it had switched to 47 per cent light (going down) and 42 per cent heavy (going up). Its export structure, Japanese planners will point out, has therefore in this decade been broadly similar to the stage that had been reached by most West European countries in about 1928. Since 1928, every West European country has gradually switched into the more "modern structure" of putting much less emphasis on "light industrial" exports (of which textiles have almost always been the main element) and much greater emphasis on exporting of heavy industrial goods. As witness the table below:

PERCENTAGE OF TOTAL EXPORTS

	Light Industrial		Heavy Industrial	
	1928	1959	1928	1959
Britain	50.7	18.3	30.5	66.1
Switzerland	54.3	25.1	27.6	66.7
Belgium	42.9	26.9	33.2	55.9
France	44.1	21.9	22.6	52.5
Italy	37.5	26.5	16.5	43.0

Most successfully of all Germany had reached 41.6 per cent light and 26.2 per cent heavy even by 1900; by 1959 it had reached 14.7 per cent light and 73.8 per cent heavy, a slightly "more modern proportion" (in terms of industrial exports only) even than the United States.

Japan's official Foreign Trade White Paper for last year was quite brutal in drawing attention to the way in which Germany made a quicker and earlier switch into heavy industrial exports than Britain:

The (different) speed of adjustment of the export structure of these two countries greatly affected later developments . . . in particular it is well known that this became an important factor in leading the British economy into a long-term stagnation. Special attention must be given to this point on the part of Japan, which still depends greatly on textile products.

And one can be quite sure that special attention will be paid to it, for the Japanese are convinced that in the second half of this century the underdeveloped countries will sweep into the export markets for light industrial products, and not only for natural textiles. When your correspondent asked one Japanese which newly developing country he most feared, the answer was unexpected: "In thirty years perhaps all of them, with China of course hanging over all; but in the next few years I think one main challenger may be Spain." Others that were mentioned were Formosa and Hongkong.

This idea of encouraging development of to-morrow's export industries, rather than concentrating entirely on today's possibly evanescent ones, is a deliberate feature of Japan's short-term policies, and not just one of its vague long-term aspirations. As one example of the statistical and planning techniques employed: income elasticities of demand for various items in the main markets of the world are studied with loving care, and this trend of world demand is then checked against what is called Japan's "specialisation index." (This term can best be explained by an example: if 5 per cent of total world trade is in chemical goods and 5 per cent of Japan's exports are chemicals too, then Japan's specialisation index for chemical goods would be one.) When world demand is rising especially heavily for some particular item, Japan's industrial planners get very worried if Japan's "specialisation index" — and thus share of world exports — for that item is not concurrently going up too. On the other hand, if Japan's specialisation index is already high for something for which world demand is not rising, the planners are not at all sorry to see that industry — even if it is currently a good exporter, such as (e.g.) tractors are for Britain — gradually dwindle.

Thus Japan's Economic Survey for 1959–1960 noted with satisfaction that in a wide range of articles for which world demand was then rising, Japan's specialisation index had increased also. These booming exports included most forms of machinery, other metal goods (as distinct from metals themselves), made-up clothing (as distinct from textile piece goods), vessels, automobiles (where admittedly Japan's specialisation index is still well below unity), and some forms of plywood and wooden products. On the other hand, the survey noted with almost equal satisfaction:

Among the items on which Japan is beating a retreat with regard to specialisation are those goods which are manufactured through comparatively simple processes and are in poor demand like yarn and cotton fabrics hitherto exported mainly to underdeveloped countries. They also include chemical fertiliser, pottery, glass products and bicycles.

But it added as a warning note:

Declines in specialisation indices are also registered for many chemical products and metals. This is quite noteworthy, for the world's demands for chemical products and metals are on the upgrade.

Following upon this sort of remark, government measures for encouraging greater output of the chemical products indicated as desirable will be stepped up.

In part, these government measures may take the form of winks and nods passed along Japan's extensive "old boy" network. (As Sir Norman Kipping and Mr. J. R. M. Whitehorn put it, perhaps with rather polite understatement, in their excellent report on Japan to the Federation of British Industries last year: "The very intimate and manifold connections at all levels between government and industry are a most important factor in the attitudes and policies of both.") But the government also has some powerful positive strings to its bow. They can include the exemption from corporation tax on profits from a new product for an initial period, extraordinary depreciation allowances (which can sometimes be very extraordinary indeed), readier permission to firms in a growth industry to import technological know-how, as well as very tight protection against foreign imports while the infant industry is being built up. And, as a most important point: if domestic demand for these industries' products grows in the meanwhile, thus giving them further encouragement to expand, that will be regarded as the happiest development of all.

This last remark leads into another vital difference between official attitudes in Britain and Japan. In Britain the government almost automatically assumes that any "excessive" increase in domestic demand necessarily causes exports to shrink, because the extra demand sucks goods into the home market; British officialdom discounts the argument of some industrialists that increases in home demand help exports by enabling manufacturers to utilise to the full the economies of modern mass production techniques. In Japan — instead of assuming that the industrialists' argument is either always wrong or always right — they set their adding machines to work to find when and whether it has proved true in each particular case. And from this springs calculation of what Japanese planners have called "the export and industrial estrangement coefficient" in various parts of their economy — another term that economists in Britain have never learned to use.

In 1950, for example, machinery accounted for 16.2 per cent of Japan's industrial output but only 10.5 per cent of its industrial exports; so machinery was calculated to have an export estrangement coefficient of 10.5 divided by 16.2, which equals 0.65. By 1959, by contrast, output and exports of machinery happened to have risen to a level where they accounted (coincidentally) for exactly 28.9 per cent of both Japan's industrial output and its industrial exports, so

EXPORTS (by Value)

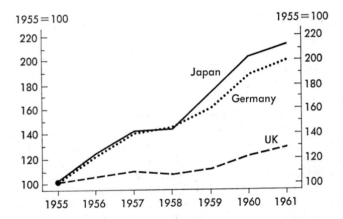

by then machinery had an estrangement coefficient of one. This, in other words, was one group in which exports had proved to go up more than proportionately as domestic demand had expanded. And the blunt fact is that the same trend has been observed in Japan in most of the "modern" industries on which increases in domestic demand within an expanding economy have recently been most heavily concentrated.

This would not be true in all countries with different schedules of marginal domestic demand; for example, in America marginal demand in an expanding society might well be mainly concentrated on services, which would often use up labour in forms of employment where they could not add to exports at all. But the situation is different when marginal domestic demand is concentrated on industries with a high rate of capital-intensiveness, in which productivity therefore increases sharply with mass production and in which it has been

proved (by those adding machines again) that qualitative improvements and investments in modernisation go forward most swiftly in
time of high prosperity for the industries concerned (so that a country
must be considered to be particularly well placed to follow expansionary policies when marginal domestic demand falls heavily upon industries with great scope for complicated technological advance). . . .

GREGORY GROSSMAN

Innovation and Information
in the Soviet Economy*

█N THE SOVIET VIEW, technological progress is not only virtually
synonymous with human progress, but is also an overriding national
goal and a major element of legitimation of Communist rule in Russia.
From Lenin's "communism equals Soviet power plus the electrification
of the whole country," through Stalin's injunction to his subjects to
"master technology," to Khrushchev's and Kosygin's "construction of
the material-technical base of communism" — each additional machine
or kilowatt, every just-trained engineer, has been identified simultaneously with yet another forward step on the direct historical path to
social perfection and human bliss as well as with the strengthening of
the internal and external power of the Soviet state. The "world-
historic victory of socialism over capitalism" is assured, we have been
repeatedly told, because socialism (Soviet-style, of course) removes
the obstacles to the full productive use of man's ingenuity and crea-
tivity and is capable of planning and organizing the productive forces
of society for unstinted technological advance and, hence, economic
progress.

A consequence of this approach has been the elaboration of a new
social technique: the routinization of economic growth. This is to
say, virtually everything connected with the process of economic

* From Gregory Grossman, "Innovation and Information in the Soviet Economy," *American Economic Review* (May 1966), Vol. L, No. 2, pp. 62–72. Reprinted by permission of the author and of the *American Economic Review*.

growth — the accumulation of society's saving, capital formation, education and training, invention, research and development, technical modernization and innovation, dissemination of technological information, and (last but not least) the massive take-over of technology from abroad — has been centrally organized and planned and subjected to standardized, repetitive, routine methods and procedures. The technique is not exclusively Soviet or Communist; some of the just-cited functions have also been routinized for some time elsewhere; for instance, research and development in large "capitalist" corporations or the defense and space programs of major Western governments have also been in large measure routinized. But its comprehensiveness and extent within the national economy are distinctly Soviet-style.

In the present paper we shall be concerned with only one aspect of the routinization of growth in the Soviet economy: the routinization of innovation and the related problems of information. By innovation we mean something rather broad; namely, the introduction and diffusion of relatively more advanced production techniques, whether indigenously developed or not and whether the given technology is finding its first application in the Soviet Union or is already known there in practice. Innovation, as we use the word, thus comes close to the standard Soviet phrase, *vnedrenie novoi teckhniki,* often translated as "the introduction of new technology."[1] If the phrase "routinization of innovation" has the appearance of a contradiction in terms, it also reflects the dilemmas and paradoxes inherent in the planning of rapid technical progress in any "going" economy and especially within the rigid context of Soviet economic and administrative institutions.

We begin, therefore, with a few words about that context. The economy is centrally managed by means of detailed output and input targets assigned to enterprises and intermediate entities. Nearly every material producer good of importance is centrally allocated. Short-term planning aims at (1) mobilizing production resources to the utmost and (2) achieving minimal consistency between production capacities, output targets, and supply allocations. In the event, this consistency is quite poorly achieved. Labor, however, is deployed largely through a free market (a major exception being that the mobility of collective farmers is administratively restricted). Investment — which has in recent years accounted for something like one-third of GNP — is nearly entirely centrally planned and controlled. Its pur-

---

[1] This phrase, however, does little justice to its Russian counterpart. The verb *vnedriat'* bears the connotation of an organic process (to implant, to cause to take root), while *tekhnika* embraces both the technique or technology of production and the physical equipment that embodies it.

pose is not only to propel the steady and rapid expansion of the country's productive capacity in the desired directions, but also to serve as the chief vehicle for the introduction of modern technology into the economy.

Prices for producer goods are administratively set (or, at least, approved) according to complicated principles and procedures which may have their rationale but in any case do not purport to seek our either scarcity or equilibrium levels. Given also some other aspects of the Soviet economic system, especially materials allocation, the result is that for most important producer goods demand exceeds supply and the usual phenomena of a seller's market prevail.

From the early days of the Plan Era until July, 1957, and again since October, 1965, industry has been formally organized according to the "branch" ("product-line," "ministerial") principle; i.e., the enterprises belonging to a given branch of industry have been subordinated to the corresponding ministry (earlier, commissariat), usually regardless of their geographic location. Between 1957 and 1965, the "territorial" principle of industrial organization obtained — most enterprises were subordinated to regional economic councils (sovnarkhozy). The organizational "partitioning" of the Soviet economy is important for our inquiry because it tends to determine (1) the pattern of information flow and (2) the structure of what Peter Wiles has called "subordinate autarky"; that is, the tendency of each administrative level to be self-sufficient. The latter phenomenon, conditioned by the system of success indicators and by the prevalence of the seller's market, appears in the form of either "departmentalism" or "localism," and, together with the tendency of communication lines to coincide with those of authority, creates the malignant situation known in Soviet parlance as "departmental barriers" — the failure of enterprises or higher organs to effectively communicate or cooperate with each other.[2]

As we might expect from the opening observations of this paper, technological information of all kinds and from all sources is avidly gathered, assiduously translated, processed, and compiled, and aggressively distributed. The volume of technical publication is enormous. Throughout the Soviet period, highly organized efforts have been made to import technology from the more advanced countries in the form of stray information, systematic documentation, production processes, prototype equipment, and live advisers. The All-Union Institute

[2] For further information on the structure and functional characteristics of the Soviet economy and on its prices, the reader is referred to [2] [9] [11] and [16].

for Scientific and Technical Information (*VNITI*) is unique in the world in the range and thoroughness of its collecting and publishing activities, although it is only one of many Soviet organizations devoted to this end.[3] Commercial secrecy as practiced under private enterprise is not supposed to exist (will the current efforts to raise the role of profit in the Soviet economy tend to revive it?) but departmental jealousy and what might be called subordinate secrecy (concealing one's true capacities from one's superiors) are practiced widely. Lastly, much technical information is also dispensed, often in directive manner, in the form of input-output coefficients ("norms") for planning, technical specifications and standards, and the like.

Much more complex is the picture with regard to economic information. As we have noted, producer goods prices are poor representations of the goods' relative scarcities for either the short or the long run. Now that state enterprises are about to begin paying interest on their fixed and working assets, capital will be carrying a price in current cost accounting as well as in planning, but it may be doubted that the rate — or, more correctly, the many "branch" and special rates — will accurately reflect the social marginal opportunity cost of this factor.[4] Land remains unpriced, though some other natural resources will supposedly soon bear rent charges. The exchange rate is of doubtful fidelity. Farm prices, even if somewhat more sensible than before, are still a country-wide crazy quilt. The wage structure does make some sense, but only with reference to supply and demand in the labor market — a circumstance from which Soviet labor was supposedly liberated by the advent of socialism.

For day-to-day production decisions, the most important economic information consists of plan targets, supply allocations, and success indicators. Both short-term and long-term planning rest on an enormous flow of statistical data, most of which is probably superfluous and in any case costly to collect and often of doubtful reliability. More important, while it forms the basis for all the planning in the traditional — centralized and "manual" — way, the information generated either in intrafirm bookkeeping or in hierarchical reporting is poorly

[3] See [13, pp. 73–76] for a concise account of such organizations. This study by Peter Knirsch is so far the only systematic inquiry into Soviet planning of technical progress published in the West.

[4] Cf. [6, esp. Chap. 11].

[5] Recent analyses of the Soviet use of the rate of return in choosing among alternative technologies will be found in works by Bergson [2, Chap. 11] and Collette [7, Part III].

suited to either management decisions[5] in the firm or to the prospect of mathematized planning at the top. Surely, at the enterprise level, and even considerably above it, there is little reliable indication from economic (as against administrative) signals of the socially most desirable directions for investment, as things now stand. Another serious defect is the very inadequate state of interfirm communication — lack of technical catalogues, advertising, salesmen — which makes it difficult to know what goods are actually or potentially available for use in production.

Perhaps even more inimical to technological progress and economic growth than the dubious quality of economic information generated by the Soviet eonomy is the lack of appropriate motivation for innovation at the enterprise level. The problem has been treated in the Soviet literature at the greatest length; we have had occasion to discuss it in this *Review* several years ago.[6] Complex in its many details, the matter is essentially quite simple: given the success indicators and the system of bonuses to management, the "taut" plans, and the "ratchet principle" of raising plan targets on the basis of most recent performance, management has little to gain and much to risk by espousing new products or processes. Besides, any change in the routine runs into innumerable bureaucratic obstacles at all levels. Hence, widespread aversion below to anything new; i.e., a reluctance to act innovatingly on information that more than offsets the commercial secrecy of the market economy.

It must be noted that machine-building enterprises are also prey to this phobia of innovation. Thus, precisely the industry which in the Western market economy, through its sales campaigns, is responsible for much of the diffusion of innovations, in the Soviet Union has the opposite role of imposing technical conservatism on itself and its clients. Accordingly, it has been machine building that has been the chief beneficiary of various schemes to reward managerial and technical personnel responsible for innovation — especially since 1960 — and to relieve the costs (and, thus, prices) of new products of expenses incurred at the development stage.[7] The Soviet literature does not

[6] [10]; see also [16, pp. 167–71] [19, Chap. 9] [3, p. 86].

[7] On these schemes for the "stimulation of new technology" see [1, pp. 98 ff.; V. Markov in *Planovoe khoziaistvo* (hereafter *P.Kh.*), 1960] [6, English text in *Problems of Economics,* III] [10; E. Slastenko in *P.Kh.,* 1964] [2; A. Basistov in *Voprosy ekonomiki,* 1964] [5; and *Ekonomicheskaia gazeta* (hereafter *E.G.*), Jan. 20, 1965, p. 37].

give a strong impression that these schemes have as yet been markedly successful in lessening resistance to innovation.[8]

Of course, much — and in the earlier period, most — of what is technically new enters the Soviet economy by being embodied in newly built plants, where the dead hand of the present has not yet appeared. By now, the Soviet Union possesses an enormous establishment for the design of new (or redesign of old) production facilities. In 1963, there were some 1,300 so-called "project-making" organizations (engineering design bureaus); in late 1965 they employed over 450,000 persons and had an aggregate budget of 900 million rubles (*Pravda*, Dec. 8, 1965, p. 5). For reasons of space we cannot inquire into their operation. Suffice it to say that the project-making organizations have been under much attack in the Soviet literature over the years because of their slowness to innovate on the drawing boards, among other things. Doubtless, the fault is not entirely with the subjective qualities of their engineering personnel; they have had to contend with inadequate economic signals, faulty incentives, and a refractory, overcentralized system.

Insofar as it has been overcome, the resistance to innovation at enterprises and in project-making organizations has been overcome in large measure by continuous administrative pressure from above. Crucial to its success are the communication channels through which it is transmitted — a problem to which we shall return toward the end of this paper in the context of the recent reorganization. But now we turn our attention to two of the most distinctive Soviet institutions in the field of technological progress, "uniform technological policy" and "the plan for the development and introduction of new technology."

UNIFORM TECHNOLOGICAL POLICY

A frequently cited concept, uniform technological (or technical) policy (*edinaia tekhnicheskaia politika*) is also a most elusive one. We know of no rigorous definition of it in the Soviet literature. Often it merely refers to the dictator's whim in technical matters or to the particular technological hobbyhorse that the given author is riding. Insofar as it does have substantive content, the concept of uniform technological policy amounts to the centralized determination and mandatory enforcement of the technological aspects and parameters of a production process. This may refer to the basic characteristics of

---

[8] But, not unexpectedly, these schemes may have aggravated conflicts of interest between innovators and production personnel within enterprise; cf. Basistov, *loc. cit.*, pp. 31–32.

the process (e.g., thermal or hydraulic power generation, type of railroad traction, automation), its main technological parameters, the types and varieties of required equipment, standardization, typical size of plant, degree of vertical integration in production, etc. An example will be found in the Resolution of the 1959 Plenum of the Central Committee CPSU which selects many dozens of technological processes in virtually all branches of industry and transport for high-priority attention [17, pp. 501 ff.]. No doubt even starker examples could be culled from the early years of Soviet industrialization.

That something like the notion of a uniform technological policy should have evolved in the U.S.S.R. is hardly surprising. It is, first and foremost, a corollary of the central planning of investment, especially where economic advance has been seen largely in technological terms to begin with. Second, investment has to be supported by specific materials allocations, which has also been highly centralized in Soviet practice. That is to say, technological specifications determine precise material requirements, which cannot be honored except at the top. Third, under Soviet conditions, the necessary linkages with other industries can be properly handled only at a very high level. Fourth, centralizing technical decisions at the center is presumably an economical way of utilizing engineering and other scarce skills. Thus, A. Kostousov, chairman of the State Commission for Automation and Machine Building which was created in 1959 expressly to lay down a technological policy in that area, wrote soon after assuming his new post:

[Technological progress requires] uniformity of technological policy in machine building. There cannot be isolated technological policies in Riasan', Minsk, Moscow, or Leningrad provinces in regard to, say machine-tool building. The coordination of technological policy is a most important task at the present stage. It will allow to save the efforts of scientists and engineers, to eliminate unnecessary parallelism and duplication, and to create the conditions for the developing the most progressive technology in all branches of machine building.[9]

On the other hand, we may well ask how feasible — under actual Soviet conditions — would have been the decentralization of basic technological decisions given the inadequate motivation, the absence of reliable economic signals, vagueness in regard to decision rules, and — we must add — far from perfect identity between the goals and values at the center and at the economic periphery.

To be sure, insofar as we know, the central authorities have not

9 *Kommunist,* 1959:8, pp. 11–12; cf. *idem* in [18, pp. 108 ff.].

had the benefit of much better economic parameters or much more precise decision criteria than those available to their subordinates. They, too, have tended — perhaps even more consciously — to mistrust internally generated price-cost information and to put their faith in more strictly technological criteria and into imitation of foreign practice. The latter, particularly, seems to have been an important criterion — both for want of others and as a convenient hedge for the individual decision-maker against the risk of being accused of deciding wrong. After all, American (or German, or British) technological solutions could hardly be wrong! And besides they are already at work. Where the central organs, however, have indeed had a clear advantage over the periphery is in their overview of the physical requirements of the whole investment program. This, of course, has only tended to support the notion of uniform, centrally-determined technological policy — even if in the event the requisite consistency and coordination have apparently been minimal.

Nor is much known as to the roles of various planning bodies and political organs in this connection. There is little doubt, however, that the abolition of the ministerial structure in 1957 adversely affected communication along branch lines and thus militated against innovation insofar as it depends — as it largely does in the U.S.S.R. — on planning and administrative pressure from above. The progressive multiplication of the State Commissions for individual industries between 1957 and 1962, and even the enhancement of their authority in matters of technological policy in 1962–63, seems to have more complicated than strengthened planning along branch lines. These difficulties have provided the main reason for a return to the formerly discredited ministerial (branch) system of industrial organization.[10]

In sum, uniform technological policy has been both reality and mirage in Soviet practice. It has certainly been a reality in the sense that huge industries have been built up on the basis of particular technologies. But the economic wisdom of these technological solutions has been quite uneven, and often probably insufficiently or inefficiently investigated in the first place. Moreover, the very goal of technical uniformity itself may have been irrational where economic conditions require a variety of technical solutions; witness the patent case of agricultural machinery. But seen on its own terms and with all the technological biases to which it has been prey, uniform techno-

---

[10] The implications of the 1957 reform for economic growth were discussed by us in [10, pp. 70–71]. A useful and concise Soviet analysis of the implications of branch and territorial partitioning may be found in Birman's booklet [4, pp. 49–64]. Knirsch gives a good account of the many organs engaged in planning technological advance in the U.S.S.R. [13, pp. 76 ff.].

logical policy in the U.S.S.R. seems as often as not to have been unattainable. Even within individual industries this has often been so owing to conflicts of personal or departmental interests, bureaucratic empire building, "departmental barriers," materials shortages, resistances to innovations, and all the other facts of Soviet economic life. It has frequently lacked continuity — or has continued for much too long (as in the case of traditional emphases on coal, steel, or railroad steam traction). As we shall presently see, it has not been effectively supported by the expressly-designed "plans for the development and introduction of new technology." And there seems to have been relatively little connection between technological policies in different industries.

**PLANS FOR THE DEVELOPMENT AND INTRODUCTION
OF NEW TECHNOLOGY**

Though far from being the only vehicle of technical progress in the Soviet economy, these plans have been the chief formal documents through which the authorities have been trying to carry out technological policy in industry and construction. Begun in the late 1940's, they are constituent parts of annual economic plans (and only of the annual plans) on each level, from the union government down to the individual enterprise. Unlike production plans, at the higher levels these plans do not aggregate the provisions of those at lower levels but rather select items of requisite importance. In recent years these measures have been a rather varied assortment, falling under six main rubrics: (1) Directives for the mechanization and automation of production processes and the introduction of advanced technology; (2) directives for the development and production of prototypes of new, important machines and articles; (3) directives for the most important research, development, and experimental projects; (4) a list of obsolete machinery, devices, etc., whose production is to be terminated; (5) directives for quantity production of new kinds of industrial products; and (6) a statement of the requirements of materials, equipment, etc., for the implementation of this plan.[11] The last provision dates only from 1962; financial requirements were included in the plans for new technology also for the first time only in that year.

Soviet sources leave little doubt that the plans for new technology are among the least effective or successful in the industrial sector of the Soviet economy. Year after year, the nominal fulfillment of the

---

[11] The fullest description of the plans for new technology will be found in [8]. A brief historical sketch is in [14, pp. 135 ff.], while the situation in the early years is described by Sokolov in *P.Kh.*, 1951:6.

union-level plan for new technology is of the order of 50–60 percent [17, p. 728] [18, p. 264] (Grishin in *Pravda*, Nov. 22, 1962). Even this may overstate the real effect in that the percentages refer to proportions of the number of items (projects) carried out or completed; there is accordingly a tendency to carry out or complete — whatever this may mean — the smaller items (projects) first for the sake of a better record. The reasons for the poor fulfillment record are many. Those most frequently cited are the lack of support with materials allocations (even since 1962), lack of financial backing, and the usual resistances to innovation.

But the plans for new technology seem to be very poorly drawn up to begin with. They are on a strictly annual basis with little if any reference to any long-term projections, let alone plans, of technological development. The selection of items and projects seems to be unsystematic, even chaotic, and with little carry-over from year to year. There is little coordination between this aspect of the annual plan and such important aspects of it as those pertaining to production, labor, supply, costs, and profits. For that matter, there is little coordination between the various parts of a plan for new technology.[12] Notably, few projects in the plan are supported by any kind of economic justification, and those that are tend to be those for which bonuses to the innovating personnel are to be paid, which renders the economic calculations suspect from the start. And so forth.[13] Perhaps it is just as well that the plans for new technology tend to be only half-fulfilled.

One can consequently appreciate all the more the intense search for institutional improvement, especially in regard to innovation and growth. The following passage, by L. Gatovskii, the recently-appointed director of the prestigious Institute of Economics of the U.S.S.R. Academy of Sciences, underscores the issue:

Under the conditions of the present-day scientific revolution and of the competition and struggle between the two world systems, the planning of scientific and technical progress must, objectively, be the leading link of the whole system of national economic planning. Yet, hitherto, this link

[12] In a similar vein, it was alleged by no less an authority than Kostousov (*Pravda*, Aug. 28, 1959) that the planning of machinery output for the Seven-Year Plan (1959–65) proceeded without reference to the investment plan.

[13] Criticisms of the plans for new technology are legion. To cite a few almost at random: [17, *passim*; 18, *passim*; G. I. Samborskii in 15, pp. 268–83; P. Abroskin in *P.Kh.*, 1961:3; I. Kasitskii in Kommunist, 1961:2; A. Pliner in *P.Kh.*, 1962:10; N. Semenov in *Pravda*, March 23, 1962; G. Kozlov in *E.G.*, 1965:46, p. 6; L. Gatovskii in *E.G.*, 1965:48, p. 5]. For analysis once again refer to Knirsch [13, pp. 88 ff.].

has perhaps actually been the most lagging link in the whole complex of national economic planning and in the whole system of material incentives for production.[14]

In a society as rich in paradoxes as is the Soviet, the area of technological progress and innovation contains its aliquot share. Everywhere in the U.S.S.R. the technologically most advanced and most backward are to be observed side by side. There is centralization of the highest order and at the same time failure to achieve some of the putative advantages of centralization; for instance, surprisingly modest progress has been made in the field of industrial standards.[15] Or there has been so far remarkably little progress in automation, despite an impressive scientific base and the absence of the institutional features that allegedly hold back automation in decentralized, pluralist economies.

Soviet technical achievements are generally not in dispute; it is the paradoxes by which the outside observer is fascinated and for which he seeks explanations. To be sure, many of the instances of lingering technical backwardness have their economic justification, if not historical explanation, in factor proportions (although on this score the foreign observer may be more generous than the domestic critic).[16] But as often as not Soviet contrasts have little economic rationale: their explanation must be sought in motivational, organizational, and institutional causes. We have already had reference to some of these, particularly those pertaining to quality and transmission of information, incentives, and the methods of drawing up plans for new technology. We now return to the concept of routinization of innovation.

The routinization of innovation on a national scale presumably means: (1) forecasting of technology for a substantial period, say a decade; (2) an economic methodology for selecting among technological alternatives, supported by projections of economic parameters; and (3) an organizational set-up to realize the desirable innovations. All three are much easier listed than accomplished. Although fore-

[14] *Loc. cit.*

[15] Cf. [20] [12, pp. 67 ff.]; V. Agranovskii in *E.G.*, 1961:9, pp. 26–27; V. Boitsov in *Izvestiia*, July 9, 1964; editorial in *Pravda*, Feb. 6, 1965; V. Tkachenko in *P.Kh.*, 1965:7. On the economics of industrial standards generally see Brady [5, Chap. IV]. Soviet problems in the area of industrial standards seem to rest on such institutional conditions as "departmental barriers," which block or delay agreement on specifications, and the opposition by producers, who dislike standards because they impose a quality constraint to quantitative plan fulfillment.

[16] Cf. S. Kheiman [1, pp. 136 ff.].

casts of technological progress are notoriously uncertain and risky, this part may be the least difficult in the Soviet case. In the recent past and for the near future the Soviet Union could and still can set its sights largely on the technology already developed and applied in the other industrial countries; thus fortunately avoiding much of the uncertainty attendant upon the projection of technological progress. Offsetting this advantage is the rigidity of the Soviet economy which resists adjustment occasioned by earlier faulty projections.

For lack of space, we shall not discuss here methods of economic choice among technological alternatives, except to note that for a long time these methods — and the corresponding informational requirements — were neglected in the U.S.S.R., although there is now a strong revival of interest in them among Soviet economists.

Much attention has lately been focused on the organizational side, thanks to Mr. Khrushchev's frequent tinkering between 1957 and 1964, and his successors' economic reform of October, 1965. Here we find many fundamental dilemmas. Should the locus of innovative initiative and activity be primarily centralized or decentralized? What are the informational implications of each alternative? If primarily centralized, what should the formal economy-wide organization be? If decentralized, how are particular and social goals to be reconciled? How to best ensure appropriate motivation and the right incentives?

To take up first the centralized alternative, which is of course the traditional Soviet approach: The "territorial" principle of organization, as we have seen, severs the vertical, "branch-specific" lines of communication and thus impairs the transmission of information and pressure for technical advance and innovation. Khrushchev's attempts to establish a complementary structure of branch organs (State Commissions) to deal with dynamic aspects of planning hopelessly complicated and confused things. We have now (October, 1965) witnessed a reversion to the ministerial (branch) principle of industrial organization, although the authors of this reform must have been fully aware of its sins. But the problem is not thereby solved. How intimately integrated should planning for innovation be with planning for current production? If they are closely combined, the day-to-day pressures of production management will tend to deflect energies and attention from long-range matters, following a kind of Gresham's Law of Planning. If they are separated, the vertical lines of communication will remain at least partly impaired. How formidable will the new "departmental barriers" prove to be? In the past, innovation that cuts across industry lines has had a particularly hard time of it. (The slow progress of automation may be partly explained this way.)

More fundamental is the problem of inserting planning for innovation into the rigid, Soviet-style system of planning and management. This system rests heavily on routine, repetition, minimal disturbance, stability; it resists all new departures. But — as the sorry record of the "plans for new technology" amply shows — the routinization of innovation can be achieved only by at least partly deroutinizing other aspects of planning, especially that of production and supply. Can it be done in a centralized system? Does Soviet-style planning at all permit of a "delicate moving balance between order and innovation"?[17] Or does it allow only gross, discrete, forced injections of innovation into an otherwise inert order?

The reforms of October, 1965, do not constitute much of a decentralization, in our opinion, despite a few steps in that direction (which is not to say that they may not eventually lead to substantial decentralizations). Unexpectedly, the most significant such step relates to investment (rather than to current production): by 1967, some 20–25 percent of all gross fixed investment in industry will presumably be undertaken in a decentralized way. Uniform technological policy is reasserted, but enterprises are called upon to exercise initiative and to innovate within its framework.[18] In the past, decentralization of investment decisions on an even much more modest scale has been handicapped by the rigidities of the highly centralized environment, especially when it came to obtaining the necessary materials.[19] Since the system of materials allocation and other centralist features are being retained, it is not clear how the much-expanded decentralized investment will now manage to fare better. Nor is it clear by what mechanism uniform technological policy will be enforced without, presumably, squashing decentralized initiative.

The irony is that, in the Soviet case, the imperative for innovation, on the one hand, and the severe obstacles with which innovation has to contend (including many of the inadequacies of information), on the other hand, derive from essentially the same root cause: the extreme historical urgency for the amassing of industrial power combined with the logic of preservation of political control by the authoritarian regime. The Soviet system is not unique, of course, in facing such grand dilemmas or such grandiose ironies. It will be interesting to see how unique will be its solutions.

[17] The phrase is Brady's [5, p. 108].

[18] See Kosygin's speech, *Pravda*, Sept. 28, 1965, and related materials; also, Gatovskii in *E.G.*, 1965:48, p. 5.

[19] We have analyzed this problem at some length in [21].

REFERENCES

1. Akademiia nauk SSSR, Otdelenie ekonomicheskikh, filosofshikh i pravovykh nauk, *Sotsial'no-ekonomicheskie problemy tekhnicheskogo progressa* (*Materialy nauchnoi sessii* . . .) (Moscow, 1961).

2. Abram Bergson, *The Economics of Soviet Planning* (New Haven, 1964).

3. Joseph S. Berliner, *Factory and Manager in the USSR* (Cambridge, Mass., 1957).

4. A. M. Birman, *Nekotorye problemy nauki ob upravlenii narodnym khoziaistvom* (Moscow, 1965).

5. Robert A. Brady, *Organization, Automation, and Society* (Berkeley, 1963).

6. Robert W. Campbell, *Accounting in Soviet Planning and Management* (Cambridge, Mass., 1963).

7. Jean-Michel Collette, *Politique des investissements et calcul économique: L'experience soviétique* (Paris, 1965).

8. S. D. Fel'd, *Planirovanie razvitiia novoi tekhniki* (Moscow, 1961).

9. Gregory Grossman, "Industrial Prices in the USSR," *A.E.R.*, May, 1959, pp. 50–64.

10. ———, "Soviet Growth: Routine, Inertia, and Pressure," *A.E.R.*, May, 1960, pp. 64–72.

11. ———, "The Structure and Organization of the Soviet Economy," *Slavic Rev.*, June, 1962, pp. 203–22.

12. S. A. Kheinman, *Ekonomicheskie problemy organizatsii promyshlennogo proizvodstva* (Moscow, 1961).

13. Peter Knirsch, "Die Planung des technischen Fortschritts," in Osteuropa-Institut an der Freien Universität Berlin, Wirtschaftswissenschaftliche Veroffentlichungen, Band 22, *Planungsprobleme im sowjetischen Wirtschaftssystem* (Berlin, West, 1964).

14. I. G. Kurakov, *Nauka i tekhnika v period razvernutogo stroitel'stva kommunizma* (Moscow, 1963).

15. Nauchno-issledovatel'skii ekonomicheskii institut Gosekonomsoveta SSSR, *Nepreryvnost' v planirovanii i pokazateli gosudarstvennogo plana* (Moscow, 1962).

16. Alec Nove, *The Soviet Economy: An Introduction* (New York, 1961).

17. *Plenum TSentral'nogo komiteta Kommunisticheskoi partii Sovetskogo soiuza 24–29 iunia 1959g, Stenograficheskii otchet* (Moscow, 1959).

18. *Plenum TSentral'nogo komiteta Kommunisticheskoi partii Sovetskogo soiuza 13–16 iulia 1960g, Stenograficheskii otchet* (Moscow, 1960).

19. Barry M. Richman, *Soviet Management* (Englewood Cliffs, N.J., 1965).

20. G. Vvedensky, "Industrial Standards in the USSR," *Institute for the Study of the USSR: Bulletin.* Oct., 1965, pp. 26–32.

21. Gregory Grossman, "Gold and the Sword," in Henry Rosovsky, ed., *Industrialization in Two Systems: Essays in Honor of Alexander Gerschenkron* (New York, 1966).

ANTON KLAS

Economic and
Administrative Steering*

THE DISCUSSION on the steering system in the national economy has reached the stage where the problem is bound to arise: should we continue to steer the economy by administrative measures, or change over to a system of economic self-regulation? There is no easy answer to this question. It involves an enormous complex of complicated problems especially of practical nature. However, new branches of science, in the first place economic cybernetics, have thrown new light on these problems and enabled us to distinguish between relevant aspects of it from a point of view which has commanded little attention so far. The purpose of this article is to look at the problem of regulation from this cybernetic point of view.

In an economy steered by the market mechanism, producers get a steady flow of information about the needs of society. This information is coded in the form of prices. If the price of a commodity deviates from its previous position relatively to other prices, the producers are economically induced to increase or reduce the production of the commodity in question. Thus, prices are steering orders, based on a large amount of data about the various individuals' needs within the framework of the economic laws of distribution in an economy regulated by the market mechanism. It is important to note that the market mechanism produces this steering information individually for every single commodity; it does not work by means of global quantities. The market mechanism works out information about the movements of millions of products, it solves systems of equations with an enormous number of variables.

It is obviously beyond the capacity of any administrative system to perform such a complicated task. Even if it were equipped with sufficient technical tools, it could hardly gather quickly enough the data which must constitute the basis of the steering orders. Thus, steering by means of administrative orders must necessarily be much

* From Anton Klas, "Economic and Administrative Steering," ed., tr., Lars Posholt, *Economics of Planning* (1965), Vol. 5, No. 1–2, pp. 87–91. Reprinted by permission of *Economics of Planning*.

simpler than steering by the market. If part of the steering is performed by administrative measures while another part is left to the market mechanism, the problem arises how to coordinate these two systems of regulation. If coordination fails, the systems are jamming each other. For each system, the steering informations of the other system represent a noise which must be filtered away.

The disturbing influences of the marked mechanism on administrative regulation can be eliminated most simply by paralysing the prices. If prices are kept stable through administrative stipulation, they cease to bring information about the consumer's situation. Nevertheless, administrative steering cannot do without prices, because it cannot, at least for the time being, distribute the results of production in any other way but one involving prices (wages, remunerations etc.). Therefore, the paralysis of prices is not absolute. Since prices still have some economic functions, they must be changed from time to time. But this is done at much greater intervals than in a market economy. During these long intervals prices cannot be adapted to the consumer's situation.

Insofar as steering by means of the market is paralysed, the economy must, of course, be steered through administrative measures. But the administration, powerful as it may be, is unable to follow the wishes of millions of consumers and all the various possibilities of production. The only way out is to simplify matters. Instead of steering the production of every single commodity, the administration steers by means of aggregates and global indicators. The less the administration is prepared for the complicated task of steering, the more it is compelled to choose only very simple global indicators. The effect of this fact on the steering process deserves careful consideration.

In the first place, it should be stressed that through the use of global indicators, a substantial amount of information is lost. An order formulated in terms of a global indicator may be carried out in a great many different ways. Thus, producers who get their orders only in global form, without sufficient specification, have a substantial freedom to choose what to produce. The assortment of commodities produced need not, therefore, correspond to the society's needs. The fundamental feedback from consumption to production, on which the very character of production as a meaningful human activity depends, is disturbed. Increased uncertainty of decision causes increased entropy in the system. In other words, the volume of information decreases, and therefore the possibilities of steering are reduced.

This impoverishment of the information link affects consumption in general, not only that of the individual consumer. All production is, at the same time, consumption. Therefore, producers, too, find themselves in the position of consumers. If the producer's chances to satisfy the needs of production are reduced, his ability to fulfil his productive task is reduced also. This results in difficulties in the relations between suppliers and receivers, stagnation of co-operation and specialisation, etc. The consequences of such a situation are increasing stores of raw materials and other means of production on the one hand, and of unsold commodities on the other hand.

A further consequence is this: Since prices are fixed, the quality of commodities is changed instead. In fact, this is price change, even if it is of a somewhat special kind. Of course, "constant price" is an illusion if the quality of the commodity changes. Prices do actually change, much more than what is generally realized, but the change occurs in a much less desirable form than necessary.

It follows that the outcome of our present campaign for higher quality of production does not exclusively depend on the moral standards of workers and controllers of production. These factors on which attention is chiefly concentrated, should certainly not be neglected, but the fundamental causes of poor quality are to be found in the system of administrative steering of the production process. The struggle for better quality must, therefore, begin in this sector. Otherwise, better quality is bound to remain a pious wish.

Since the administrative system of steering cannot distribute the commodities available for consumption without making use of prices, the producer's material incentives must be incorporated into the system in a way consistent with prices, that is, as wages, profits etc. In this field, the administrative system makes use of the form of economic self-interest which has been developed by the market mechanism, and is intimately connected with it. Here, we have a paradox, an intrinsic inconsistency of the present steering system. The incentives which constitute the chief moving force of production, are connected with prices, but the formation of prices is not dependent on the laws of market mechanism.

As a consequence of this inconsistency, the producer's interest may deviate from society's interest. Producers pursuing their economic self-interests, need not necessarily tend to satisfy the most urgent needs of society. If prices are kept fixed during long periods of time, they do not reflect those needs. Thus, producers are induced to satisfy in the best possible way the needs of some fictitious consumers. Since this inconsistency is a result of the present system's basic features, it cannot be wholly eliminated within the present framework. As long as the system remains fundamentally unchanged, the administration can cope with disturbances only by specifically administrative measures, i.e., orders and prohibitions. If disturbances increase, the size and the power of the administrative apparatus must be increased still more.

In order to avoid stagnation of production, prices cannot be allowed to have a decisive influence on production. In the first place, the connection between the size of invested funds and the producer's self-interest must be eliminated. Such indicators as productivity, economical use of resources, effectivity etc. are very often considered as the most suitable instruments of steering. In fact, they are no steering instruments at all; they are indicators of economic progress. Suppose, it is found necessary to reduce production in some particular branch of the economy. This reduction cannot be made dependent on reduced productivity, or increased costs, or less economical use of resources in the branch concerned. Rather, these indicators should always show progress, regardless of whether production is increased or reduced. Therefore, steering cannot be carried out by means of these indicators, important as they are.

But there is a factor which may be increased or reduced, and whose variations do entail corresponding variations of production. This factor is the size of invested funds. Increase of funds results, under otherwise equal conditions, in increased production; and vice versa. The steering mechanism of market economy connects, in fact, the producer's self-interest with the size of these funds, not with the costs of production. Whether production is advantageous for him or not, depends on the relation between the profit and the invested funds. But of course, this relation is significant only if prices are determined in an appropriate way. If their movements are frozen, the relation mentioned looses its significance. Under such conditions, it is not surprising that the concepts of profit and invested funds are hardly interpreted as economic concepts any more. As a matter of curiosity, the names are still in use, but they are not used in a consequent way. For example, what we call "fund of wages," is simply wage cost.

This is also the reason why economic self-interest is defined in terms of such indicators as productivity etc. Under the conditions of administrative steering, the fact that these indicators are given the role of economic incentives, is tantamount to a permanent production campaign.

The non-existence of connexion between the producer's self-interest and the size of invested funds produces more far-reaching consequences than is generally realized. Firstly, the number of half-finished projects and the size of stores of raw materials, unsold goods etc. are growing beyond the possibility of control. More important still, even funds actually invested may be wasted. If, in addition, prices are fixed in the wrong way, it becomes impossible to find an objective yardstick for comparison between alternative investment projects. It is also made difficult to evaluate in a critical way different conceptions concerning the development of the national economy as a whole. These problems can be solved only in connection with a solution of the problem of steering.

Neither administrative steering nor the apparatus which is carrying it out, can be eliminated by a pen's stroke. Nevertheless, the only way out of the difficulties mentioned above is to adopt consequently the system of economic steering and to make use of its automatic mechanism. Only if and in so far as this change of system will be successfully carried out, will parts of the administrative apparatus loose their functions, and thereby it will become possible to reduce its size effectively. But the question is not only about the administrative apparatus. It is also necessary to re-evaluate the style of work created by it.

PART TWO

PATTERNS AND PERFORMANCE

INTRODUCTION

Most students and economic textbooks are likely to concentrate on comparisons of the growth rates of the Soviet and U.S. economies. This information is increasingly more readily available and forms a popular topic for news media and political debates.[1] These readings, seeking to supplement rather than duplicate such material, draw their illustrations of patterns and performance of demand and command systems from a larger sample. Besides, comparison of the two economic systems, important though it is, does not permit broader generalizations about command and demand mechanisms. Indeed it tends to reduce the variety of economic systems and policies to an overly restrictive and misleading dichotomy in which the polar cases are confused with the possible realities.

Historically annual rates of economic growth in the U.S.S.R. have been over 6%, as compared to about 3% in the U.S.

Whether Soviet growth rate in the last few years has been as low as 2½% as the C.I.A. has estimated, or almost zero as Professor Warren Nutter believes, or close to 4% as Professor Nove thinks,[2] there is little doubt that it is much less than in the previous years and decades. The 5% rate of growth of the American economy since 1960 is among the highest in U.S. history and so far shows no signs of slackening. This is all the more impressive considering that the

[1] For one excellent source see Stanley H. Cohn in U.S. Congress, Joint Economic Committee, Hearings, *Dimensions of Soviet Economic Power* (Washington, D. C., 1962).

[2] See Alex Nove, "2½% and All That," *Soviet Studies*, July 1964, pp. 17–21; and Comments by Stanley H. Cohn, Murray Feshback and Nove's reply in *Soviet Studies*, January 1965, pp. 302–325.

U.S. is trying to curtail agricultural output so as to reduce its farm surpluses while the Soviet Union and other Communist countries in general are in desperate need of expanding their agricultural output.

Catching up with the West is a popular slogan of Russian policy-makers. But its meaning is neither simple nor clear. The Soviet Union can already be considered on par with the U.S. in military power. If her rate of economic growth again becomes and stays larger than that of the U.S., then at some time in the future, depending on the differences of these rates, she would catch up and eventually surpass the U.S. in total annual output. Since the U.S.S.R. has a larger population than the U.S. and the two populations are growing at about the same rate, it will take longer for the U.S.S.R. to catch up and surpass the U.S. in per capita output. Even then the stock of wealth, total as well as per capita, would be vastly different in the two economies. That stock has been accumulated over a much longer period of growth in the U.S., which did not suffer significant destructions of this capital as occurred in the Soviet Union during several wars and civil wars. If one makes these comparisons between Soviet bloc countries of Eastern Europe and NATO countries of Western Europe, the prospects of the former catching up with the latter, even in total output, in the foreseeable future are much dimmer.

Wolfgang Stolper and Karl W. Roskamp show how East and West Germany, sharing the same culture, history, and work habits and many socio-economic features showed different economic results under the two polar versions of command and demand. From 1950 to 1958, total output as well as per capita output rose much faster in West than in East Germany. Standards of living rose even faster in West Germany. These trends appear to be continuing, though organizational reforms and the elimination of the drain of professional and skilled youth to West Germany seem to be improving the performance of the East German economy.

Amlan Datta examines the achievements of Russia and Japan, two countries with long records of very rapid economic growth and concludes, "Economic salvation can be attained by diverse paths . . . people committed to an ideology tend to believe that some particular set of institutions is essential to economic growth. But here as elsewhere history has a way of bypassing narrow convictions."

That Marxism or Communism does not necessarily necessitate centralized economic planning was demonstrated by Yugoslavia almost a decade ago. Jaroslav Vanek discusses the rapid growth generated by the decentralization of economic decision-making and reintroduction of many of the features of a market economy. This experience seems to have contributed to the strengthening of the promarket viewpoints in other Communist economies. These views have found their most forceful expression in the abandonment of Stalin's economic heritage by Czechoslovakia in 1964.

The recent reforms need not necessarily solve Czechoslovakia's problems. The unwillingness of the party leadership to let prices fluctuate freely, the shortage of trained, experienced, and enterprising managers, the likely emergence of monopolies out of "prospective industrial amalgamations" (which in turn will strengthen the case for government controls on prices and output), are some of the factors that make the future of this experiment uncertain. According to Vaclav Holesovsky, the new reforms, instead of loosening the control of the party, are likely to lead to more party activism among the workers. Under command planning, enterprises tended to hoard labor and capital. "Under the New Model, any shift toward efficiency in management would be accompanied by dismissals and the attendant problems of transition to new goals."[3] The unwillingness of the regime to introduce unemployment insurance (because of their unwillingness to admit the existence of unemployment) may cause frictions and labor militancy. This, in turn, could lead to tighter political controls.

[3] Vaclav Holesovsky, "Czechoslovakia's New Economic Model: Problems and Prospects," *Problems of Communism*, Sept.-Oct. 1965, pp. 41–45.

WOLFGANG STOLPER AND KARL W. ROSKAMP

East and West Germany:
Some Comparisons*

BY 1955, industrial production as a whole in East Germany had increased to 127.1 per cent of 1936, and by 1957 to 140.7 per cent (both computed in 1936 prices). Production in the Federal Republic rose to 197.8 per cent. In 1950 prices, industrial production in East Germany rose to only 113.4 per cent by 1955 and to 125.6 per cent by 1957. The 1950-base index of the Federal Republic shows that by 1955 there was already an increase to 198 per cent. The aggregate showing of the Federal Republic was undoubtedly and spectacularly better.

Two comments should be made on the interpretation of these figures. First, the population increase between 1936 and 1955 was much greater in the Federal Republic than in East Germany. For this reason alone, the tremendous increase in industrial production officially claimed in East Germany as compared with the Federal Republic is not credible. Even adjusted to a per capita basis, by 1955 the 1936 index of East Germany had risen to only 114.1 per cent of 1936, compared with the rise for the Federal Republic's 1936-base index to 155.1 per cent. In 1950 prices there is virtually no growth at all in per capita production of East Germany between 1936 and 1955, while the growth of the Federal Republic's new index compared with the old one is hardly smaller than when calculated in 1936 prices.

It may be objected that West German growth reflects basically the fact that West German industry blossomed out following the

* Reprinted by permission of the publishers from Wolfgang Stolper and Karl W. Roskamp, *The Structure of the East German Economy* (Cambridge, Mass.: Harvard University Press), pp. 239–241, 263–264, 266–267. Copyright, 1960, by the Massachusetts Institute of Technology.

currency reform of 1948 and by 1950 had already reached a level 10 to 13 per cent above 1936 while East German industry did not really start to grow until 1950, when the First Five Year Plan was inaugurated. True, the level of production of East Germany in 1950 was only two-thirds to three-fourths of the 1936 level, an admission which is not, of course, officially made. (The index of industrial gross production of the Zone [that is, without East Berlin] given in the Statistical Yearbook of the Federal Republic shows for 1950 a level of 85 per cent of 1936.) However, the planned economy has developed vigorously since 1950. Thus it might be argued that the most relevant comparison is the rates of growth since 1950.

Before making such a comparison, it should be pointed out that it is by no means clear just what such growth comparisons are supposed to prove. Usually growth rates of the United States and the Soviet Union are compared — to give the most frequently used example — in order to prove either that the Soviets will or will not catch up with the United States or to show that the failure of consumers to be better off in the planned economy was a necessary sacrifice to achieve high growth rates in the economy, to lift a backward country out of stagnation, to break the chains of feudalism, and to release the productive powers of a sleeping economy.

Whatever may be said about such comparisons for underdeveloped countries, the reasons usually given to justify an interest in growth rates rather than in absolute levels do not apply to East Germany. It was not a feudal country in any sense; and culturally, sociologically, and historically it did not differ significantly from the area of the Federal Republic. If anything, it was more radical in politics, had more Socialists and Protestants, and about the same number of "feudal" barons and backward peasants. Certainly the cure of communism was not needed to establish the conditions for growth.

Economically, the East German area was not backward either. . . . Backward areas do not pioneer in the production of synthetic gasoline or synthetic rubber, or establish world leadership in optical goods or national leadership in electrical goods.

Hence even a growth rate no different from that in West Germany would prove at best that with sufficient labor inputs the planned economy can produce something which after all was denied only by a diehard minority of self-appointed guardians of free-market economy purity.

Between 1950 and 1955 the growth of East German industrial output was about 70 per cent compared with a growth in the Federal

Republic of 75 per cent (1936 prices and old index, respectively). In terms of 1950 prices and the new index the growth was slightly larger for both areas.[1]

On an aggregate level, the gap between East and West Germany continued to widen between 1950 and 1955. The aggregate growth rates of the West were undoubtedly better, but on a per capita basis, the picture is substantially modified. Per capita output in East Germany (the population of which had declined by 1955 to 97.6 per cent of its 1950 level) rose to about 173 per cent by 1955. Per capita production of the Federal Republic (the population of which had increased by about 5 per cent between 1950 and 1955) rose to 166.5 per cent. (Both figures refer to the old index for the Federal Republic and the index in 1936 prices for East Germany.)

This rise could be considered an achievement for East Germany. But its true meaning cannot be discussed without reference to the fact that the base with which East Germany started was substantially lower (both in the aggregate and on a per capita basis) than that of the Federal Republic. Furthermore, the substantial increase in the industrial labor force, the composition of the growth, and the development of other sectors should all be considered. . . . [I]t may be stated that agricultural output undoubtedly increased in the Federal Republic between 1950 and 1955 and between 1936 and 1955. In East Germany there was a decrease between 1936 and 1955, although no marked change occurred between 1950 and 1955. Construction particularly of housing undoubtedly lagged catastrophically in East Germany. There is evidence that the growth of industrial production in East Germany is limited by unsatisfied import needs for raw materials and, possibly, insufficient investments; in the West any possible stagnation comes only from the demand side and can therefore more easily be remedied. . . .

PER CAPITA GROWTH IN EAST AND WEST GERMANY

That industry has in the aggregate grown substantially faster in West Germany than in East Germany compared both to 1936 and

[1] The reason growth since 1950 is larger when measured in 1950 prices, while compared with 1936 it is larger when measured in 1936 prices, is that the important price changes occurred before 1950 and were largely completed by that year. For example, comparing 1955 with 1936, wool prices rose much more than rayon prices, but the total increase was before the Korean war.

to 1950 has been established beyond reasonable doubt,[2] the one exception being coal mining. If the East German regime were not so entirely absorbed in its own propaganda, it could of course point out that this should be expected. After all, it could be argued, the population of the Federal Republic increased about 27 per cent between 1936 and 1955 while that of East Germany increased only 11 per cent; and the Federal Republic has absorbed increasing numbers of emigrants from East Germany since 1949, thus reducing the East German population. Hence, it might be argued, per capita changes are more significant.

Because the old and new index of the Federal Republic differ only insignificantly, only the new one, which is less favorable to the Federal Republic, will be presented. But for East Germany, calculations in both 1936 and 1950 prices must be shown. Only the West German classification will be discussed in this section.

In West Germany, per capita production was substantially restored to the 1936 level in all industries by 1951. Only the mining (and gas) sector was still 3 per cent below prewar. By 1955 all per capita production was substantially above prewar, the least increase being shown by mining, the most by electricity and investment goods. The average per capita increase was 55.5 per cent above 1936, with mining, basic materials, consumer goods, and food, drink, and tobacco being below and electricity and investment goods (which, however, also includes passenger cars) being above the average. Per capita production, which in 1950 was still 9 per cent below 1936, was 7 per cent above it in 1951.

The story in East Germany is quite different. In 1936 prices, aggregate per capita production exceeded the 1936 level only in 1954, and in 1950 prices only in 1955. But in 1950, mining was already 9 to 16 per cent above 1936. In 1950 prices, basic and production goods and investment goods passed the 1936 level in 1953. Neither consumption goods nor the output of food, drink, and tobacco had reached the 1936 per capita level by 1955, or, for that matter, by

---

[2] The comparison with 1950 is made because adequate East German data became available with this year and because in 1950 the First Five Year Plan was started. But this comparison date is not as meaningful in the Federal Republic. The logical starting date in the Federal Republic is 1948; and what corresponds to the Five Year Plan in East Germany is the currency reform of 1948 and the whole range of policies from derationing to (at a later date) increasing use of monetary policy — policies usually associated with Ludwig Erhard.

1957; and in 1955 manufactured consumer goods were still more than 40 per cent below the 1936 level.

In 1936 prices the story is somewhat more favorable to East Germany. Basic and production goods definitely reached their 1936 level in 1951. But the only other significant change is that food, drink, and tobacco were about 3 per cent above 1936 in 1955. Aggregate per capita production reached the 1936 level between 1953 and 1954.

Since 1950, per capita developments in the two parts of Germany are almost the same, although in aggregate development East Germany lags slightly. But as recovery started earlier in the Federal Republic and was much more vigorous, a comparison of the growth since 1950 is of only limited significance. It is particularly interesting, however, that only in mining (including gas), and *mirabile dictu,* consumer goods and food, drink, and tobacco was the per capita development in East Germany faster than in the Federal Republic. I need not labor the point that the comparatively fast growth in consumer goods industries was, to vary a classic phrase of Winston Churchill's, primarily due to the fact that East Germany had so little to grow from. In addition, we are dealing here with per capita production of manufactured consumer goods and not per capita consumption. It is known that East Germany exports a substantial portion of its manufactured consumer goods output. Even at the end of rapid growth the East German consumer is still worse off than before the war. The comparison of per capita growth in East Germany and the Federal Republic for 1955 compared with 1936 is, except in mining and basic and production goods, unfavorable to East Germany, to say the least. [See Table 96.]

OUTPUT PER WORKER—EAST AND WEST GERMANY

Finally, a comparison of output per man in the Federal Republic and in East Germany will serve to put developments in perspective. The comparability is unfortunately far from perfect, but the data are sufficient to furnish a good idea both of developments since 1950 and of the absolute magnitudes involved. In 1955, output per worker in all industries (including electricity and gas) was DM 6,687 in East Germany. In the Federal Republic, total output per worker in 1955 (excluding electricity and gas) was DM 13,125. These figures are comparable to the extent that they are both based on West German prices. But our calculations do not include indirect taxes, and West German figures do. Hence industry-by-industry figures would be somewhat more relevant. In basic industries output per worker in East Germany in 1955 was DM 9,750; in West Germany (where the coverage is narrower and the electricity output with its high output per worker, as well as mining, is omitted) it was DM

TABLE 96 — INCREASES IN PER CAPITA PRODUCTION BETWEEN SELECTED YEARS, 1948–1955, MAJOR INDUSTRY GROUPS, WEST GERMAN CLASSIFICATION, WEST AND EAST GERMANY

	West Germany (1936 prices)			East Germany 1950–1955		East Germany compared with West Germany, 1950–1955, 1950 = 100	
	1948– 1955	1950– 1955	1948– 1953	1936 Prices	1950 Prices	1936 Prices	1950 Prices
	(1)	(2)	(3)	(4)	(5)	(6)	(7)
Mining and gas	170.2	132.0	154.9	145.4	147.3	110.2	111.6
Electricity	210.8	165.3	168.1	151.3	151.6	91.5	91.7
Basic and production goods	305.2	166.2	236.0	162.5	158.7	97.8	95.9
Investment goods	411.3	212.2	288.7	215.8	212.6	101.7	100.2
Consumer goods	327.2	154.4	275.3	169.3	167.1	109.7	108.2
Food, drink, and tobacco	269.9	156.8	237.8	178.7	186.1	114.0	118.7
Total	304.0	169.6	241.2	174.5	176.5	102.9	104.1

13,812. Since indirect taxes are not significant at that level, it is fair to say that productivity in West Germany in 1955 was almost certainly one and a half times the level in East Germany. Western output in mining alone was DM 9,323.

In investment goods (which so far as coverage is concerned, are completely comparable), output per man in 1955 was DM 11,253 in West Germany and DM 6,241 in East Germany. Here, too, indirect taxes are probably insignificant. It is fair to estimate West German productivity in 1955 as about three-fourths higher than in East Germany. For consumer goods industries and food, drink, and tobacco, indirect taxes play a larger role; hence the figures must be taken with caution, particularly as the coverage, too, is not identical. Nevertheless, whatever adjustments are necessary, there can be little doubt that output per man is substantially higher in West Germany than in East Germany.

For West Germany, data for output per hour worked and per production worker employed are available. But no comparison with East Germany is possible. The official East German data on output per production worker and output per person employed in industry refer only to socialized industry; and they are vitiated by the fact that they are based on gross production in *Messwerte*. Since it is

TABLE 97 — OUTPUT PER EMPLOYED PERSON IN 1955, WEST AND EAST
GERMANY, MAJOR INDUSTRY GROUPS, IN 1950 PRICES (DM)

	West Germany	East Germany
Total production	13,125	6,687
Basic industries	13,812	9,750
Mining	9,323	. . .ᵃ
Investment goods — metalworking	11,253	6,241
Consumer goods — light industries	9,775	4,109
Food, drink, and tobacco	33,734	9,875

Sources: For East German calculations, employment figures from *SJDDR*, 1956, p. 245, were used. The 1956 figures differ from the same data given in the *SJDDR*, 1955, p. 121. No details are given about the extent to which industries have been reclassified. West German figures are derived from *Neuberechnung* and indices of productivity per employed person, *SJBR*, 1957, p. 233.

ᵃ Impossible to calculate mining without including gas.

now even officially admitted that this is a meaningless and even harmful figure, it has not been considered. The data are summarized in Table 97.

AMLAN DATTA

Japan and Russia: Notes
towards a Comparative Study*

BOTH Russia and Japan started on a career of rapid industriali-sation in the closing years of the last century. Compared with some Western countries both were "late starters." Both attained in course of time strikingly high rates of growth. It is interesting, therefore, to attempt a comparison of these two contemporary experiences. A detailed study of this nature will involve repetition of much that has

* From Amlan Datta, *A Century of Economic Development of Russia and Japan* (1963), pp. 181–184. Reprinted by permission of The World Press Private Ltd.

been said in the preceding pages. Only a few brief and suggestive hints are offered below.

Both Japan and Russia as late-starting countries have been in a position to borrow extensively from the more advanced technology of the West. This has been one of the important factors in their unusually high rates of industrial growth.

In Japan the economic transformation of the country was already started under the *shogun* in the last years of the Tokugawa era. But a new leadership soon took over. This new leadership was not radically different from the old in its social roots. In Russia industrialisation first started under the guidance of the tsarist government within a semi-capitalist framework. The Bolshevik revolution of 1917 brought into power a revolutionary leadership. This leadership was ideologically and otherwise cut off from tradition, and particularly from the peasantry, to a much greater extent than was the case with Japan. The difference in the quality of leadership in the two countries had economic consequences of some importance.

The Japanese leadership succeeded to a much greater extent in increasing agricultural productivity without revolutionary changes in the organisation of agriculture. In this respect the performance of the Soviet government was very unsatisfactory. While radical changes were forcibly carried out under the Stalinist regime, there was relatively little improvement in agricultural productivity.

Both in Russia and in Japan a good part of the "surplus" for investment in economic development was secured from the agricultural sector. But the institutional framework through which this was accomplished differed widely in the two cases. The conflict between the political authority and the peasantry was markedly more bitter and long-drawn-out in post-revolutionary Russia than in Japan after the Mejii restoration. Both in Russia and in Japan farmers were faced with adverse price movements in the period between the two World Wars, and in both cases the peasants suffered much as a result. But in Russia this was more the result of a deliberate policy adopted by the government, while in Japan it was primarily the consequence of market forces and business depressions.

In the Soviet Union, once the civil war and consequent disorganisation of the economy had been overcome, the growth of large-scale industry proceeded rapidly, but not without a sharp set-back for small-scale industry. In Japan the two categories of industries developed together in a process of mutual adjustment. Light industries were the first to develop in Japan and heavy industries lagged behind for a time. In Russia development of heavy industries, particularly iron and steel, started relatively early, although in the period prior to World War I light industries, such as textile, were among the leading industries. After the revolution, and particularly in the period of the Five Year Plans under Stalin, emphasis moved sharply in the direction of heavy industry. In Japan too, as the economy assumed a militaristic character, particularly in the 1930's, a shift of emphasis in the same direction became unmistakable. In both countries spells of rigour and hardship have at last yielded place to rising trends in standards of living, particularly noticeable since the mid-1950's.

The Japanese economy depended for its development far more on foreign trade than the Russian economy. This was more or less pre-determined by the relative resource endowments of the two countries: the influence of ideology was perhaps only marginal in this respect. While Russia expanded eastwards in search of new resources, Japan crossed her national boundaries and moved for a while more obviously in the direction of imperialism. However, the situation has changed markedly after World War II.

The Japanese economy, functioning on the basis of a predominantly private-enterprise system, and geared to the world economy through a more extensive network of foreign commerce, has been susceptible to a greater extent to cyclical fluctuations of economic activities. However, recessions have generally been milder and booms more vigorous in Japan than in most other leading capitalist countries. The Soviet Union, with her planned system, has avoided similar alternations of booms and slumps. Another result of this difference of systems in the two countries is that concentration of power in Japan manifested itself typically through the rise of the *zaibatsu*, the big business houses, receiving favours and assistance from the government, while in the Soviet Union a corresponding phenomenon was the growth of a managerial stratum working in close collaboration with the party in power. A system of social security sponsored by the state arose earlier and assumed a more comprehensive character in the USSR, although the collective farmers could not share much in its benefits. The Japanese substitute for this till recently was a kind of paternalism, individually and imperfectly administered in the main, extending to the lower levels of the economy.

In Japan, with her far greater density of population, a policy of population control was perhaps called for even earlier and has actually been adopted and vigorously pursued after World War II. In the Soviet Union government policy has aimed at encouraging growth of population. Differences in resource-population ratios in the two countries have also had pervasive influence on the industrial structure of the two countries. In these respects other countries in Asia face situations generally more comparable with Japan than with the USSR.

Thus, Russia and Japan, while sharing a few common points as late-starting countries and in so far as military considerations have had a large measure of influence on the patterns of their economic development, display, at the same time, profound divergences springing from differences in natural endowments, qualities of leadership and economic systems of the two countries.

These divergences as well as the common points between the two countries serve to emphasise one central truth. Economic development, like salvation, can be attained by diverse paths. If a country wants to have rapid development, it must, indeed, fulfil certain basic requirements. It must, for instance, build up an adequate system of training and education; it must so reorganise its agriculture, industry and financial institutions as to make possible the raising and investing of a substantial "surplus" from the economy; it must have some reasonable arrangement for coordinating development in different sectors. But these requirements can be satisfied in a number of alternative ways. While the educational system of a country aspiring to rapid development should inculcate a sense of the dignity of labour and promote interest in science and technology, neither protestantism nor dialectical materialism nor any other special doctrine is essential to industrialisation. Again, there is a significant contrast between the economic organisations of the two countries under study. The difference between the respective ways in which agriculture is organised in Japan and Russia is very great. In industrial organisation, too, there is a similar contrast between the two countries. People committed to an ideology tend to believe that some particular set of institutions is essential to economic growth. But here as elsewhere history has a way of by-passing narrow convictions. The range within which choice and experimentation are possible in economic development is not unlimited; but it is fairly wide, as the cases of Russia and Japan studied side by side help us to realise.

JAROSLAV VANEK

Yugoslav Economic Growth and Its Conditions*

INTRODUCTION

THE PURPOSE of this panel is to discuss economic growth in three Communist countries, and the specific purpose of this paper is to do so for the Yugoslav economy. More so perhaps than for the other two cases considered, that of Yugoslavia requires particular attention to be given not only to the purely statistical aspects of growth but also to the over-all economic conditions generating and conditioning this growth. Indeed, the Yugoslav experience is without precedent in a number of respects; it resembles closely neither the Western nor the Eastern centrally planned prototype of economic organization. Rather — at least in the minds of the Yugloslav planners and lawmakers — it is an attempt to combine the allocational efficiency of largely competitive markets and highly decentralized decision making with the distributional efficiency of collective ownership.

Thus our task is not so much to present a systematic verbalization of the very abundant statistical information presented in the Yugoslav yearbooks and other statistical material, but rather, once the salient points about the growth have been made, to state the principal characteristics of the Yugoslav economy and to perform a few global tests of its dynamic efficiency. Two sets of such tests can be conceived of. On the one hand, because the economic system in Yugoslavia since before the war has passed through three distinct stages, certain rough correlations can be established between the type of economic organization and the rate of growth of the economy. On the other hand, in the most recent period when the economy assumed its specifically Yugoslav form, certain hypotheses bearing on efficiency can be formulated on the basis of a comparison with other Communist countries more closely adhering to the Russian type of allocational patterns.

I am confident about the accuracy of the data presented here.

* From Jaroslav Vanek, "Yugoslav Economic Growth and Its Conditions," *American Economic Review* (May 1963), pp. 555–61. Reprinted by permission of the author and of the *American Economic Review*.

I have come to this conclusion through a summary study of the consistency of different statistical materials. Moreover, many Western economists who are acquainted with Yugoslav statistics as well as independent Western institutions seem to share my opinion. However, a thorough and independent appraisal of Yugoslav official statistics is desirable and is yet to be undertaken.

GROWTH OF THE ECONOMY SINCE BEFORE THE WAR

Only very little precise information is available concerning the state of the Yugoslav economy preceding World War II. However, even from the little there is, it can be concluded that Yugoslavia as a whole was among the poorest countries of Europe in the prewar years and very little headway, if any, was made between the two wars towards changing this situation. In retrospect, the backwardness of Yugoslavia of those years will become apparent from the fact that in 1960, when the country could compare only with comparatively poorer industrialized countries with three to four hundred dollars of per capita income, industrial production was about five times higher than in 1939; in agriculture, on the other hand, the number of tractors rose about thirteen times and consumption of artificial fertilizers almost forty times in the same period.

An approximate link between the pre- and postwar periods can be established for 1947. In that year, the economy pulled itself out of the worst of the disastrous consequences of the war; industrial output stood at about 121 per cent of 1939 and agricultural production lagged by about 10 per cent behind the average of the thirties. Thus it can be concluded that in 1947 national product was roughly comparable to that of the years preceding the war.

Beginning with 1947, far superior and more abundant statistical information is available. For reasons that will become more apparent in the subsequent section, and in order to conform to the time limitation imposed by the scope of this panel, we prefer to carry out the discussion in reference to annual averages for certain specific periods rather than in reference to individual years. There are four such significant periods: the first covers the years 1947–52, the second 1952–56, the third 1956–60, and the fourth, covering the current Five Year Plan, extends to 1965. The overlapping years of the different periods are to be understood as reflecting the fact that our data mostly pertain to average growth rates. Thus, for example, the first period will reflect the average annual changes that took place between 1947 and 1952.

In the first period, gross national product grew at an average compound rate of 2.4 per cent per annum, in the second at 8.8 per cent, in the third at 12.6 per cent, and it is expected to increase at the rate of about 11 per cent in the current five-year period. While an important discontinuity will be observed in the first period, national product having actually declined in its latter part, over the second and third period the rate of growth was remarkably stable. In the second and third periods, the growth would actually have been even more regular were it not for a rather erratic behavior of the agricultural sector, whose growth still was heavily influenced by climatic conditions.

Industrial output was not only the most stable component of the Yugoslav growth pattern, but it was also the most progressive one. While increasing from about 33 to 46 per cent of gross national product between 1947 and 1960, it grew at a rate of about 6 per cent in the first period, about 12 per cent in the second, and 14 per cent in the third. Agriculture and construction barely stood above the 1947 level at the end of the second period; however, their increase was remarkable in the third period when the former grew at over 8 per cent and the latter at over 16 per cent.

As could be expected, the high rates of growth just pointed out for the whole economy were accompanied and largely generated by a relatively high rate of capital formation. Throughout the first three periods the share of national product allocated to gross investment was fairly stable, in the neighborhood of 30 per cent. In the first period it was somewhat lower than that figure, in the second slightly higher, and in the third just about at that percentage. In the terminal year of the current Five Year Plan, gross investment is expected to stand at about 33 per cent of national product.

In the first two periods, the most important recipient of investment funds was the industrial sector, its share in the total being close to 60 per cent. The second, absorbing almost two-thirds of the rest, was the transportation sector, while the residual of about 15 per cent of the total of gross capital formation was directed into construction, agriculture, and other sectors. In the third period, the share of total investment going into agriculture has increased to nearly 20 per cent of the total, largely at the expense of a declining share of investment in industry. A similar pattern, although somewhat less pronounced, is expected to prevail in the current Five Year Plan, with industrial investment falling just short of 50 per cent of the total.

Before ending this factual exposition, some remarks bearing on the most recent situation of the last two or three years are called for.

Following 1959, a certain deceleration in the Yugoslav rate of growth is noticeable. While in the first year of that period it was fully imputable to a poor harvest, with industrial output growing faster than ever before, between 1960 and 1961 both major components of national product performed less satisfactorily, the former declining even further owing to another bad harvest, while the rate of growth of industrial output declined to about 7 per cent. In the current year 1962, the increase of industrial production seems to be comparable to the low rate of the preceding year rather than to the extraordinary growth rates of the second and third periods noted above. This then raises the question whether the targets set for industrial production in the current Five Year Plan are not too high. To answer it, we have to learn something about the possible causes of the abrupt deceleration between the third and fourth periods. We will return to this problem presently.

EFFICIENCY OF THE ECONOMY IN THE LIGHT OF CHANGING SYSTEMS AND OF INTERNATIONAL COMPARISONS

Following the second World War, Yugoslavia adopted an economic system much akin to that of Soviet Russia of that time, characterized by highly centralized administrative management of the economy, with very little reliance — if any — on the price mechanism, and only the roughest regard to an efficient resource allocation. Forced farm collectivization and compulsory state deliveries were the rule in the agricultural sector. The period corresponding roughly to this regime is defined in the preceding section as our first period.

The failure of the economy to grow at a satisfactory rate in those years, however, can be imputed only to a minor extent to the economic system. Without any doubt, political tensions that arose in the later part of the period between Yugoslavia and Russia with its satellites were the more important causes of the poor economic conditions. Trade with other Communist countries that was initially very important virtually disappeared in the years following 1948 and development credits extended by Soviet Russia were cut off.

As a result of these developments, Yugoslavia was brought to seek its trading partners and creditors outside of the Communist bloc and, perhaps more important, to make an attempt to find less rigid and more efficient forms of economic organization, better suited to its particular conditions. Abandonment of forced collectivization, the introduction of workers' councils with a high degree of economic autonomy, and a parallel political decentralization were the corner-stones of the reform.

The fundamental legislation establishing and defining the competence of the workers' councils was enacted in 1950, and the political reforms required by the new economic system followed in the subsequent period roughly extending into the second period, as defined in the preceding section. This period can be considered as one of gradual consolidation of the new conditions and also of recuperation from the disastrous situation caused by external Communist blockade of the country.

Although the significantly higher rates of growth can to some extent be imputed to the belated utilization of capacity accumulated in the preceding period, fruits of the reforms are already discernible in the second period. It must also be recognized that the results of those years would not have been so satisfactory were it not for the new trading outlets Yugoslavia found outside of the Communist bloc and, especially for the economic aid it received primarily from the United States.

But the full impact of the new regime comes to light in the third period, when expectations of the Five Year Plan were realized in about four years, and when the national product grew at a rate of nearly 13 per cent, the highest in the world during that period. It will be recalled that in those years of the latter fifties gross capital formation was no higher, measured as a share of GNP, than in the preceding two.

As the success of the third period can largely be imputed to the new forms of economic organization, a somewhat more thorough and more abstract exposition of the principal factors of that efficiency is in order. First of all, it will be observed that the autonomy given to workers' councils in individual firms carries with it as one of its effects a high degree of market competition, individual firms being free to act in different markets to their greatest advantage; the natural consequence of such a situation is an efficient allocation of resources throughout the economy. Actually, it can be shown that a fully competitive system operating under workers' management and profit sharing, all other things being equal, will lead to the same type of Paretian optimum as is usually postulated for a competitive capitalistic system.

Moreover, at least some will agree that the incentive provided by profit sharing may yield better results than a system with a competitive capitalistic labor market. Also, it can be argued – figuratively – that a corporation's stockholders will be better informed and more concerned about the working of their enterprise if they are its workers than if they are not.

In regard to the allocation of investment funds, the Yugoslav system based on both external and internal financing of projects and the current practice with respect to the former type of financing guarantees — or at least is consistent with — an efficient allocation. Here we understand by "efficient allocation" approximate equalization of the internal rates of return throughout the economy. But the public management of an important portion of the supply side of the capital market carries with it another important factor of efficiency. It can be shown that the authorities managing the short- and long-term capital markets can make savings of the economy identically equal to investment, irrespective of the level of income. In other words, if properly managed, the capital market in Yugoslavia will closely reproduce the conditions of Say's law; actually, it can do so irrespective of whether prices are flexible downward or not. Price flexibility, in turn, considered as quite satisfactory in Yugoslavia — primarily because of the absence of monopolistic elements in the labor market — can only enhance the adjustment of the economy to full employment and full capacity, in cases where mismanagement of the capital market could otherwise tend to produce a Keynesian type of unemployment.

Let us now return briefly to the mainstream of our argument and attempt to explain, or at least hypothesize, about the abrupt declaration of the growth rate that has occurred in Yugoslavia in the last two years. In the first place, it can be argued that no economy could ever hope for a prolonged rate of growth of 13 per cent with a net capital formation of roughly 20 per cent of national income. Some gradual deceleration would be only the normal thing to be expected. However, a sudden decline from 13 per cent to around half of that rate cannot be explained on those grounds.

It appears that there were other factors, some of short-run, some of long-run character, some statistical, some economic, that have to be brought in to explain this decline. It has been suggested that part of the decline can simply be imputed to the statistical definition of national income: certain services of the order of about 10 per cent of national income are called unproductive and are not reckoned as components of national income. Nevertheless, it is very likely that the income elasticity of those services is greater than unity and thus part of the deceleration could be explained in this way. Another factor that ought not to be overlooked is a rather drastic reform of producers income tax, from strongly progressive to proportional, about two years ago. Such a tax, although probably desirable in the long run, may have acted as a strong disincentive in the short run especially with prosperous undertakings, where suddenly without any increases in productivity the return to be distributed among the members of the enterprise may have strongly increased.

Finally, it will be recalled that in both 1960 and 1961 agricultural output declined with respect to the preceding year. Not only did these crop failures have a direct impact on the growth of the total gross product of the economy, but, also, as certain manufacturing industries are linked in varying degrees to the farm output, value added by those industries was lagging behind what it would have been otherwise.

With these arguments in mind, it can be concluded that the long-run rate of growth of the Yugoslav economy to be expected for the fourth period (the current Five Year Plan) is not correctly indicated by the measured rate of the past two years; the true rate may well be 2 per cent above that measured. However, it also seems quite unlikely that the actual average increase for the current period would be as high as the planned 11 per cent.

In concluding this summary account of the performance of the Yugoslav economic system, let us draw at least one international comparison: that between Yugoslavia and Soviet Russia. Using Professor Bergson's data based on 1937 constant-price valuations (in *The Real National Income of Soviet Russia since 1928*, Chapter 14), we infer that the Russian rate of growth never exceeded 60 per cent of the peak rate of Yugoslavia, realized in the third period, and most of the time it was well below that percentage. But it also will be noted, again using Professor Bergson's computations, that the Russian share of GNP allocated to gross investment never stood above that of Yugoslavia, and only in the five-year period 1950–55 the share of gross investment was about comparable, even if still somewhat lower than the Yugoslav 30 per cent. It is also in this period that the peak rate of growth of 7.5 per cent was attained in Soviet Russia.

Considering the very rough evidence we have on the comparative levels of economic advancement of Yugoslavia and Soviet Russia, it can be argued, as a first approximation, that the state of economic development of Russia in the early fifties was about that of Yugoslavia in the latter part of that decade. If this hypothesis can be accepted as correct, then, with comparable shares allocated to gross investment, an average rate of growth of 12.6 per cent must be recognized as significantly higher than that of about 7.5 per cent; and all other things but the form of economic organization being approximately comparable, it appears, as could be expected on a priori grounds, that the Yugoslav form is more efficient than the other. On a per capita basis — a measure that some might prefer — the comparison comes out even more favorably for Yugoslavia; the rates of growth thus evaluated become 11.6 and 5.8, respectively.

HARRY G. SHAFFER

Czechoslovakia's New Economic Model: Out of Stalinism*

AFTER the Communist takeover in 1948, Czechoslovakia's political and economic system was patterned on that of the Soviets and its government became as Stalinist as any in the Soviet bloc. Political and cultural control by the Stalinist party apparatus was complete; five-year plans gave priority to heavy industry at the expense of the agricultural and the consumer goods sectors; and central planning authorities left few economic details to be decided at lower echelons of the economic machinery.

Even after Khrushchev's denunciation of Stalin at the 20th CPSU Congress in 1956, Czechoslovak party leaders embarked upon the Kremlin-ordained course of destalinization with utmost reluctance and with correspondingly little effect. Long after the body of Stalin had been removed from its place of honor in the Lenin Mausoleum in Moscow's Red Square, and long after other Soviet bloc countries had demolished the outward vestiges of the personality cult, Stalin's 50-foot statue continued to tower over Czechoslovakia's capital. It was not removed until October 1962.

It is true that throughout the 1950's the centralized Czechoslovak command economy experienced considerable growth — largely because

* From Harry G. Shaffer, "Czechoslovakia's New Economic Model: Out of Stalinism," *Problems of Communism* (September-October 1965), pp. 31–40. Reprinted by permission of *Problems of Communism*.

of the forced expansion of heavy industry.[1] Yet it is questionable whether even this specious form of economic growth, achieved by sacrificing quality of production and consumer interests, took place because or in spite of the centralized planning apparatus. In any case, the growth rate of Czechoslovakia's industrial output and national income, averaging about 11 and 7 per cent respectively between 1957 and 1960, began to drop in the 1960's; both were negative in 1963.[2]

A BACKGROUND OF ECONOMIC ILLS

Of all the Communist countries, Czechoslovakia has had the longest tradition of capitalist democracy, and it entered the era of "dictatorship of the proletariat" at a considerably higher stage of industrialization than any of the others.[3] Yet in 1963 Czechoslovakia became the only industrialized country in the entire world to register a decrease in industrial output, national income and real wages.

In addition, the goods that were produced were of such inferior quality that the value of rejects reached 1.5 billion Kcs in 1963;[4] during the first seven months of 1964 defects in industrial projects cost the country 365 million Kcs.[5] So serious has this problem become that Czechoslovak observers openly admit that "quality has become the foremost concern of the party and the economic authorities."[6] Newspaper reports, radio broadcasts, countless complaints from dissatisfied customers and official statements testify to the fact that the difficulties in quality control persist. In February 1964, for instance, show windows in the East Bohemian town of Hradec Kralove displayed in "one of the most effective forms of the struggle against rejects . . . an electric shaver which did not shave, an iron which

---

[1] Official Czechoslovak sources give the 1963 National Income in *current prices* as 172,605 million Kcs (Czechoslovak crowns), as compared with 59,087 million Kcs in 1948. *Statisticke prehledy* (Prague), No. 2, 1964, p. 68 ff.

[2] *Hospodarske noviny* (Prague), No. 9, 1964, p. 3.

[3] Industry, including construction, accounted for 65.7 per cent of the Czechoslovak national income in 1948; agriculture for 22.1 per cent. According to official figures, these percentages had changed to 75.1 and 13.8 per cent respectively by 1963. *Statisticke prehledy,* No. 2, 1964, p. 68 ff.

[4] *Pravda* (Bratislava), Feb. 10, 1964. At the official exchange rate, $1 equals 7.2 Kcs. However, the present tourist exchange rate is 16.08 Kcs for $1 (*Ceteka,* Jan. 6, 1965), and Czechoslovak tourists now can purchase up to $100 at an exchange rate of 36 Kcs per dollar (Radio Kosice, March 19, 1965).

[5] Eric Bourne, *Christian Science Monitor* (Boston), Aug. 3, 1964.

[6] Adolf Rostlapil, *Hospodarske noviny,* Aug. 21, 1964.

did not iron, a cooker which did not cook, and pen knives which did not cut."[7] In 1964, too, a shoe factory in Slovakia turned out shoes whose soles fell off after only a few days of wear, although the shoes retailed for 105 crowns a pair.[8] Defective coolers used in agricultural cooperatives caused milk losses "amounting to hundreds of thousands of liters every month."[9] And the Elektrosvit factory in Nove Zamky, Slovakia, which had been granted the "Red Flag" award "in recognition of its splendid results in the fourth quarter of 1963," the next year sent 500 refrigerators to Brno, all of which, on close inspection, proved to be defective.[10]

As almost everywhere in the Communist world, concentration on capital goods production brought in its wake a great housing shortage, especially in the industrial centers. In Czechoslovakia, almost one third of all families are reported to have less than eight square meters (about 80 square feet) of floor space available per person,[11] and a poll of 1,800 young couples in the 20–23 year age group, taken in several large cities, revealed that 60 per cent of the newly-weds live with the parents of one of the spouses.[12]

The supplies of some food items (especially meat and meat products) improved considerably in the early months of 1964, eliminating some of the previous shortages, but many other consumer goods such as beer, mineral water, canned condensed milk, transistor radios, silicon raincoats, and some electrical appliances failed to meet demand.[13] A Czechoslovak writer vividly depicted the trials and tribulations of the Czechoslovak consumer in the Prague literary journal, *Literarni noviny:*

I fear becoming so used to daily calamities that I will consider it an unusual and happy occasion when there are available in places where they should be batteries, transistors, buttermilk, red beets, upholstered chairs, white lead for paint, reserved train tickets, nylon shirts, fountain pen refills and recording tape. . . .[14]

[7] Radio Prague, Feb. 21, 1964.

[8] Radio Bratislava, July 29, 1964.

[9] Radio Bratislava, Apr. 20, 1964.

[10] The award was announced by Radio Bratislava, March 7, 1964; the faulty shipment *at precisely the same time* by Radio Prague.

[11] Deputy Zdenka Dohnalova addressing the Czechoslovak Assembly on February 26, 1964. *Ceteka,* Feb. 26, 1964.

[12] *Ceteka,* June 2, 1964.

[13] Radio Bratislava, July 30, 1964.

[14] Reported by Ernest B. Furgurson in the *Baltimore Sun* of May 29, 1964.

While there is a pronounced shortage of many consumer goods, the economy continues to produce many "unmarketable" commodities. In 1963, total inventories increased by 7 billion Kcs,[15] and the total value of unsalable inventories is estimated to approximate one fourth of the country's national income.[16]

To alleviate such discrepancies, the regime changed prices of consumer goods several times in 1964, raising the prices of goods in short supply and lowering the prices of products that were not taken off the market in sufficient quantities to clear the shelves. Since price increases of some goods were at least partially offset by price decreases of others, it would be impossible, without statistical computation, to evaluate the overall effect on the Czechoslovak consumer.[17] However, a series of drastic changes decreed early in 1964 provided a definite indication that living standards in Czechoslovakia (although generally considered still the highest in the Communist world) left much to be desired. In an unusual radio and television appearance on February 7, Premier Jozef Lenart announced an upward "adjustment" of rents, hitherto subsidized by the state, "to cover approximately the costs of operation, particularly maintenance and repairs";[18] the imposition of a progressive tax on pensions of more than 700 Kcs per month; the introduction of small charges for drugs and some school supplies heretofore given out free of charge; and an increase in the prices of formerly subsidized meals for workers served in factory cafeterias.

These measures are a part of the effort of the regime to make the country live within its means; they are, moreover, an expression of the awareness that artificially maintained low prices (or high incomes) can lead to shortages and disproportions without raising overall living standards. As one Czechoslovak commentator put it:

We must take into consideration the old, well-known truth that we can only parcel out what there is to be parcelled out. . . . Even the best possible government cannot distribute what is does not have.[19]

In addition to all its other economic woes, Czechoslovakia has been suffering from a severe labor shortage. Early in 1963, in fact,

[15] *Nova mysl* (Prague), No. 3, 1964.

[16] *Hospodarske noviny,* No. 12, 1964.

[17] For the two-year period from 1961 to 1963, living costs rose more rapidly than money wages, so that *real* wages experienced a slight decline. See *Statisticka rocenka CSSR,* 1964, Prague, 1964, p. 41.

[18] Radio Prague, Feb. 14, 1964.

[19] J. Svoboda in *Pravda,* Feb. 10, 1964.

the regime termed it the underlying reason for the abandonment of the 1961–65 plan.[20] By late summer 1964, there were at least 50,000 job vacancies in a country whose population numbers around 14 million.[21]

In an effort to combat the labor shortage, the government last year decided to import a few thousand badly needed coal miners from Poland and to reintroduce small-scale private enterprise, primarily in the service trades, to tap the two million pensioners, the unemployed housewives and those members of the present labor force who are willing to engage in after-hours work. The importation of foreign workers has of course the disadvantage of increasing the number of consumers as it increases the number of producers, and it has therefore not been attempted on a large scale in Czechoslovakia. At the same time, the opening of certain service trades to private enterprise has met with rather limited success. Deterred by red tape, high license fees and the requirement to submit to supervision by a socialist enterprise, very few individuals in Czechoslovakia seem to have taken advantage of the opportunity so far, although the first partial re-privatization decree has been on the books for more than a year. In any case, since Czechoslovakia already has one of the world's highest labor-participation rates, efforts directed at a *more effective* utilization of the *present* labor force appear more promising. Towards this end, the government in 1964 started shutting down all unprofitable productive capacity; introduced special financial incentives to lure workers into such sectors as agriculture, mining and building, where the labor shortage is especially pronounced; reduced by more than 37,000 the country's administrative apparatus;[22] and offered special premiums and awards to collectives, groups of workers and even individuals who succeed in reducing the working force of an economic unit while still fulfilling the output quotas.

THE SEARCH FOR A CURE

The economy of any country may be adversely affected by events that lie beyond the control of the government. At least two such events (a political crisis and a natural calamity) left their imprint on Czechoslovakia in the early 1960's. First, the Sino-Soviet split resulted in a sharp and sudden drop of Czechoslovakia's trade with

[20] *Ceteka*, Feb. 11, 1963.
[21] Eric Bourne in *Christian Science Monitor*, Aug. 3, 1964.
[22] *Rude pravo* (Prague), Oct. 31, 1964.

China, depriving the former of a supplier of food and raw materials and a not-too-demanding customer of machinery and equipment.[23] Secondly, the severe drought of 1962 played a major role in the agricultural debacle of that year, which, compounded by the savage 1962–63 winter that temporarily interrupted transportation, was bound to leave its mark on industrial production in 1963.

Yet, however damaging these events may have been, Czechoslovak officials have not blamed them exclusively for the difficulties that have beset the economy. They have noted instead many symptoms of a lingering disease and they have applied, in piecemeal fashion, spot remedies to provide temporary relief. Most economists, however, and even key party officials soon agreed that a radical cure was needed to restore the economy to a healthy condition.

Even though Czechoslovakia's economic problems are manifold, the economists are convinced that one single systemic defect — *detailed economic planning from the center* — is at the root of the trouble, and that only the elimination of the existing planning structure will provide the fundamental cure. They advocate, therefore, a decentralization of economic decision-making, emphasis on material incentives and strong reliance on the forces of supply and demand as the principal measures necessary for a successful recovery.

Attempts to institute such reform are not entirely new in Czechoslovakia's post-1948 history. As far back as 1957, the party

[23] While Czechoslovakia's trade with China dropped severely, her total trade with foreign countries has increased. The official statistical yearbook gives the following figures:

Czechoslovak Trade with Communist China
(in millions of Kcs, FOB border)

Year	Exports	Imports
1960	787	672
1961	245	302
1962	86	184
1963	67	209

Source: *Statisticka rocenka CSSR 1964*, Prague, 1964, p. 368.

Czechoslovak Trade with Foreign Countries
(in millions of Kcs, FOB border)

Year	Exports	Imports
1960	13,982	13,072
1961	14,733	14,570
1962	15,793	14,904
1963	17,723	15,554

Source: *Ibid.*, p. 265.

Central Committee had decided that central management of "fundamental matters" ought to be combined with extended rights and responsibilities of plant managers in "current matters" and that more emphasis should be placed on material incentives.[24] On April 1, 1958, certain economic reforms were in fact, introduced; these, however, are recognized today as "halfhearted" and "rather shy steps in the direction of economically sound management of the economy"[25] and as an ineffective "compromise solution."[26]

When the 1961 plan was underfulfilled, the party first placed the blame on the decentralization measures of the 1958 reforms and, reversing its former positions, asked for the "strengthening of central management."[27] But subsequently, the 12th Czechoslovak Party Congress (December 1962) decided that henceforth all proposed economic measures must be carefully examined and subjected to public discussion. Thus an atmosphere was created in which progressive thought could flourish, allowing the debate to swing once again in the direction of greater economic decentralization. For the following two years, first timidly and then ever more frankly, the shortcomings of the prevailing system of management and planning were discussed and analyzed, and eventually there emerged a plan for a "New Economic Model."

WINDS OF REASON

In February 1963, Radoslav Selucky, a young Leningrad-trained economist, launched the first major attack against the "cult of the plan."[28] He soon found rapidly spreading support among reform-minded intellectuals. Although the opposition of the conservative officialdom, including party leader Antonin Novotny, remained strong, a conference of leading Czechoslovak economists in October 1963 openly discussed the country's economic ills and made strong recommendations for abandonment of the rigid system of centralized planning, urging in its stead increased dependence on market forces in economic management. By the year's end the discussion had spread

[24] *Rude pravo*, Oct. 18, 1957.

[25] *Pravda*, Jan. 27, 1964, and *Pravnik* (Prague), No. 4, April 1964.

[26] *Rude pravo*, Dec. 23, 1964. For a more detailed discussion of the 1958 reforms see, for instance, Alec Nove's section on "The Czech and Polish Models," in his *The Soviet Economy*, New York, Praeger, 1961, pp. 242–45.

[27] *Rude pravo*, Aug. 14, 1962.

[28] *Kulturni tvorba* (Prague), Feb. 7, 1963.

from scientific conferences and technical journals to daily newspapers and cultural and political periodicals. It soon became apparent that those who advocated a "fundamental change" in the system were gradually gaining the upper hand.

In the summer of 1964, the editors of *Pravnik* (the publication of the Law Institute of the Czechoslovak Academy of Sciences) sent a questionnaire to leading economists and lawyers asking them for their views on the "proper" system of management of the national economy. Not one single voice among those who replied defended the system of central planning under which, ever since 1948, the Czechoslovak regime had tried to determine everything from the output of hydroelectric power and steel to the production of toothpaste, ice cream and engineering graduates.[29] By 1965, university professors no longer hesitated to criticize publicly the "Stalinist model" of economic centralism and to denounce as a mistake the copying of the pre-Khrushchev Soviet system of management in a highly developed country like Czechoslovakia.[30]

Arguments in many respects similar to those propounded in the USSR by Yevsei G. Liberman[31] have been advanced in speech after speech and in article after article by the Czechoslovak reformers. As long as quantitative output is ordained from above and remains the primary achievement indicator, the argument goes, is it any wonder that managers and workers alike tend to disregard product quality and consumer demand, "stubbornly continuing . . . to produce useless goods?"[32] Is it any wonder that productive capacity is concealed to secure easily attainable targets; that it often becomes "more important to fake the fulfillment of a task than to make a real effort to achieve socially desirable results";[33] that machinery and equipment (allocated free of charge by the state) are hoarded irrespective of immediate usefulness; and that technical innovation is considered an unwise risk which, if successful, would only bring higher output quotas for the subsequent year? All in all, the economists believe,

[29] See *Pravnik,* No. 6, June, and No. 7, July 1964.

[30] See, for instance, Ladislav Tomasek, Lecturer at the Prague party college, in *Planovane hospodarstvi,* No. 2, 1965, and Benedikt Korda, holder of the Chair for Mathematical Methods at the Prague Higher School of Economics, in *Planovane hospodarstvi,* No. 1, 1965.

[31] For a discussion of Liberman's proposals see, for example, Harry G. Shaffer, "What Price Economic Reforms? Ills and Remedies," *Problems of Communism,* May-June 1963, pp. 18–26.

[32] *Pravnik,* No. 4, April 1964.

[33] *Kulturny zivot* (Bratislava), No. 48, Nov. 28, 1964.

the prevailing system of management has failed to correlate the interests of individual enterprises and their employees with those of society.[34]

Since quantitative output has proved to be inadequate as an index of efficiency, planners in several Communist countries of Eastern Europe have been experimenting with different success indicators. Expedients, such as bonuses paid for increasing labor productivity, for introducing innovations, for improving quality and for saving on scarce inputs have been tested, but all of these measures have merely further complicated the already cumbersome planning apparatus. (In Czechoslovakia, not long ago, the case of a director was reported who had to fulfill 17 indices to qualify for a bonus.[35]) Today, the progressive economists are convinced that there is only one index that would suitably measure performance and at the same time coordinate the interests of workers and directors with those of society at large: profit.

If profit is to perform these functions, enterprises must be free to seek it without interference from centralized controls over details of production. They must be allowed to decide for themselves what goods to produce and where to sell them, what inputs to use and where to purchase them, how many workers to hire and how much to pay them, what share of total net profits to distribute among employees and what share to set aside for investments intended to increase future income. To the extent to which enterprises are not free to make such decisions, to that extent profit loses its value as a meaningful measuring rod of enterprise efficiency and to that extent also the profit motive is weakened as an effective incentive towards efficient and socially desirable performance. Hence, almost by definition, the utilization of profit and of the profit motive must go hand in hand with economic decentralization and with a considerable extension of the influence of market forces over economic decision-making.

The blame for the lack of success of the 1958 decentralization measures in Czechoslovakia is now placed primarily on the failure to make profit the basic index and to link the material interest of the enterprise with it.[36] This shortcoming of the 1958 reform (apparently resulting from an ideological aversion to what then was

[34] *Rude pravo*, Oct. 17, 1964.

[35] *Kulturny zivot*, No. 48, Nov. 28, 1964.

[36] See, for instance, *Pravnik*, No. 4, April 1964, and *Rude pravo*, Dec. 23, 1964.

held to be too "capitalistic" an approach) is not to be repeated in
the mid-1960's. Although the details of the proposed changes have
been sharply debated, Czechoslovak reformers are in general agreement that profit and the profit motive must be given a meaningful
place within the framework of the socialist economy. It is also generally understood that the proposed reform will entail a diminution
of the central planning organs' economic powers and a simultaneous
transfer of such powers to the lower echelons in the productive
process and, in the final analysis, to the consumer.

THE NEW ECONOMIC MODEL

On October 17, 1964, *Rude pravo* published in a 12,000 word article
the "Draft Principles for the Perfection of the System of Planned
Management of the National Economy." The document had been
approved in September by the Presidium of the Communist Party
Central Committee and generally conforms in its thrust to the ideas
publicized during previous months by a number of economists and
in particular by Ota Sik, head of the Economic Institute of the
Academy of Sciences and member of the party Central Committee.[37]
In essence, the "Draft Principles" envisage the scrapping of detailed
economic planning from the center and propose to substitute for it
the mechanism of a market economy operating within the framework
of a broad overall social plan.

After the Presidium's preliminary approval, the "Draft Principles" were returned to the Central Committee's Economic Commission for further study. To the surprise of some observers who
expected that the dogmatists within the party would assert at that
stage their opposition to the proposals, the Commission proposed no
alterations beyond emphasizing the need for a more consistent elaboration of questions related to prices, levies, credits and the status of
the central organs. The Central Committee plenum, held, after one
postponement, at the end of January 1965, then followed suit by
issuing a resolution that approved the New Economic Model without
substantial change.[38]

After proclaiming that the existing system of detailed planning

[37] See, *Zemedelske noviny* (Prague), Feb. 1, 1964, and *Nova mysl* (Prague),
October 1964.

[38] See, "Resolution of the Central Committee of the Communist Party of
Czechoslovakia on the Main Trends of the Perfection of Planned Management
of the National Economy and on Party Work," *Rude pravo*, Jan. 30, 1965.
Unless specifically indicated otherwise, all quotes and conclusions in this section
are drawn from the resolution.

at the center had "fulfilled its historic mission" (the "Draft Principles" had characterized it as "unwieldy, bureaucratic, and obsolete"), the CC resolution proceeded to outline the new approach to economic planning and management as follows.

Greater Authority for Enterprises. The function of central economic planners is to be reduced to the laying down of "the basic proportions of production . . . and distribution." Central planning bodies and central control agencies are to concentrate their efforts on broad, long-term planning; on such important, fundamental questions as price, wage and incentive policies, and the balanced economic development of individual regions; and on the control of situations presenting "the gravest danger" of "antisocial trends" (such as, presumably, could arise if large production units were left free to exploit their monopoly status without restrictions from above). The actual management and initiative in the productive process is to be left "as much as possible" to the basic economic units or their joint organizations. Enterprises, in other words, will be free to decide by themselves or in conjunction with other enterprises all economic details within the limits of the broad outlines laid down at the center.

Profits. From their total revenues, or "gross income," enterprises are to defray direct costs of production (including expenditures for raw materials, parts, transportation, and interest on bank loans) and their "obligations to society" (*i.e.*, interest and installment payments on state investments in the enterprise and contributions to the state budget). The remainder is then to be used by the enterprise for distribution among workers and managerial personnel and for investments in the enterprise itself to enhance future income.[39]

From the part of enterprise income set aside for the remuneration of employees, basic wages will be paid out first in accordance with the overall wage policy laid down by the central planning authorities. The rest, under a kind of profit-sharing system, will be distributed among workers (and managers) at the discretion of the economic unit, presumably in the form of incentive payments and bonuses for especially deserving employees. In regard to basic wages, the plan calls for the discontinuation of leveling policies, so that henceforth acquisition of greater skills and preparation and training for more important and more responsible positions should be more

[39] Enterprises will be free to use a part of the profits for "collective consumption" (such as the building of recreation centers for employees), but since this type of consumption, formerly so much encouraged, does not seem to provide the same motivating forces as enhanced individual incomes, it is apparently being de-emphasized at present.

adequately rewarded. In this manner, a worker's income is to be related to his own qualifications and performance as well as to the economic achievements of his "intra-enterprise unit"[40] and of his enterprise as a whole. Since enterprise profitability is assumed to result from both efficiency in production (low production costs) and concentration on quality and assortment reflective of consumer demand (salability), a direct link is thus presumably established between the interests of individual workers, economic enterprises, and society at large.

Investment. In the sphere of investment, too, the central organs are to lay down only the overall policy: they are to decide upon "the basic orientation of investment policy, the big development programs, and the conditions and criteria for the effectiveness of sector investments." Otherwise, guided by considerations of profitability, enterprises will be responsible for their own investments. They will finance them out of their own funds or through bank loans. Contrary to prevailing practice, all debts will have to be repaid with interest, out of future earnings.

Prices. If the market mechanism (rather than an all-wise planner) is to allocate resources so as to meet consumer demand, arbitrarily set prices must be replaced by prices which reflect relative scarcity. The party leadership, however, is unwilling to let prices fluctuate freely, in accordance with the market forces of supply and demand. The new economic model calls therefore for three types of prices: fixed, "limited," and free. Raw materials and all basic products such as coal, electricity, steel, wheat, etc., will carry fixed prices set at the center, but, similar to the price reforms instituted in East Germany in April and July 1964, costs and demand are to be given due consideration and prices are to be changed whenever changed conditions indicate the necessity for such action. "Limited" prices, apparently applicable to a wide variety of commodities, will be permitted to fluctuate within prescribed limits. Free prices, affecting initially only a small sector of the consumer goods industry, will be

---

[40] These so far undefined "intra-enterprise units" appear to be modeled after the "economic units" of Yugoslavia, where attempts have been made to determine the income of economic units within large enterprises and to tie workers' incomes to the financial achievements of these units. Since in large enterprises one individual worker is too small a particle to influence the achievements of his enterprise, it is believed that incentive would be enhanced if workers' incomes were tied to the accomplishments of the departments in which they work, rather than to the entire enterprise.

left to respond, without limitation, to the forces of supply and demand.

Enterprise Combinations. Structurally, the new economic model provides for horizontal integration of enterprises through the formation of "trusts" and for vertical integration via "concerns."[41] While the offices of the trusts and concerns will clearly represent the highest agency still directly concerned with the financial management enterprises, a precise delimitation of authority within the integrated units remains to be defined.

Foreign Trade. The foreign trade mechanism is also to be "liberalized." To motivate domestic enterprises to sell abroad, they are to have the right to keep a part of the foreign currencies they have earned. On the other hand, they will also be relatively free to purchase their supplies abroad if foreign producers can deliver them more cheaply than domestic suppliers.

Schedule of Implementation. The reformers have cautioned again and again that the major changes they advocate could not be put into effect at once. While the "Draft Principles" clearly stated that "the Central Committee can no longer wait" to *start* the introduction of the new measures, there is clear cognizance that the new system must be introduced gradually. The year 1965 is to be a period of experimentation during which some of the principles of the reform are to be tested in selected enterprises. In 1966, the "basic principles of the new system" are to be implemented in the "main branches" of the economy, even if details will still remain to be worked out later.[42]

Isolated experiments with economic decentralization involving the utilization of profit and of the profit motive were actually started early in 1964. In January 1965, the testing went into full swing. During the first half of the month, selected enterprises in the consumer goods industries began to experiment with entirely uncontrolled prices,[43] and it was announced that a freer system of prices (limited prices in state-owned factories, free prices in cooperative

[41] Horizontal integration refers to the uniting into one organization of a number of independent enterprises operating at the same phase of production (mining, manufacturing) and usually in the same line of business; vertical integration refers to the administrative concentration of enterprises functioning at several or all phases of production — from raw material extraction to the production of finished goods and often even including marketing organizations charged with distributing the commodity.

[42] *Planovane hospodarstvi* (Prague), No. 2, February 1965.

[43] *Rude pravo,* Jan. 11, 1965.

enterprises) would be tested in an entire production sector: the furniture industry.[44]

Ideological Justification. In the Communist world outlook, Marx is not merely the John Locke and the Adam Smith of socialist political and economic thought; he is viewed more in the way in which Christ is looked upon by Christianity. Hence, to be acceptable, such far-reaching changes in the system of planning and management as are incorporated in the New Economic Model first had to be justified in terms of Marxist ideology. The economic reformers have therefore consistently denied that they were "revisionists," and they refer to their experiments with various aspects of a market economy as "creative Marxism." In a hundred different ways during the past two years they have expounded the view that "in the process of the regeneration of creative Marxist thinking . . . economic theory has gradually disposed of the supposition that socialism will always continue operating under one and the same model of management,"[45] and they have attacked as "ideological prejudice" the notion that socialist production cannot be regulated by the market.[46] Finally, since planning has always been held to be the backbone of an economy structured along Marxist-Leninist lines, they keep insisting that the proposed new system "will not mean less planning but better planning"[47] and that "the effectiveness of central management will be increased by its being relieved of the task of making decisions in questions which, by their very nature, should be reserved for the enterprises. . . ."[48]

CONCLUSION

The system of detailed economic planning from the center, which may have certain merits if used to speed up the development of a backward country, has been imposed for a decade-and-a-half upon Czechoslovakia, the industrially most advanced state in Eastern Europe. Now, at long last, economic necessity and a powerful intellectual effort by a new breed of Communist-trained economists have, at least for the time being, convinced a somewhat reluctant party

[44] *Ceteka,* Jan. 4, 1965.

[45] *Politicka ekonomie,* No. 5, 1964.

[46] Quoted and discussed in *Rinascita* (Rome weekly of the Communist Party of Italy), Nov. 21, 1964. See also *Zemedelske noviny,* Oct. 7, 1964.

[47] The "Draft Principles," *op. cit.*

[48] Professor Stefan Luby, *Pravnik,* No. 7, July 1964.

leadership that complete economic control from the center is not necessarily the epitome of economic wisdom. But how well the reformers will succeed when their New Economic Model is put to the test of life is a wide open question. Few will doubt that there are very serious difficulties ahead, stemming partly from imperfections of the new scheme dictated by the necessity of political compromise, and partly from the necessarily slow pace of changing the practices and overcoming the attitudes established during long years of economic controls from the top.

To mention just a few of the more obvious problems: The party leadership will surely not be included for some time to come to go very far in releasing price formation from central control. To the extent that prices will remain centrally determined, they will reflect, in some measure at least, the preferences of the planners rather than those of the consumers; and to that same extent, profit will fail to function as a fully meaningful measure of economic efficiency. Similar defects will result if a policy of rigid wage control from the center is maintained. Other problems are likely to arise in the wake of the prospective industrial amalgamations. It is true that they may help reduce costs of production in certain cases, but they will also tend to create monopolies which, under a reasonably free price system, would find it profitable to restrain production and maintain high prices. In other words, here is another possible inducement to the government to exercise price control.

One more problem must now be mentioned — one that may, indeed, turn out to be the most serious the economists and the government will face: the shortage of trained and experienced and enterprising managerial personnel. During fifteen years of detailed economic planning from the center, the regime had little use for the skilled managerial resources the country had developed prior to 1948, nor did it see any need to train new ones. Apart from the party's established personnel policy, which rewarded political conformity and neglected skill and ability, the highly centralized system of detailed planning could virtually dispense with managers in the true meaning of the word. What it needed, and what it promoted, was political bureaucrats who could take orders and then gladly pass them on. But the New Economic Model is predicated on skillful and *enterprising* management, in other words, on enterprise directors who not only are adequately trained, but who also have a personal stake in the fulfilment of their task; in short, men who can act as entrepreneurs in the best sense of the word. Unfortunately, the government's effort to overcome the scarcity of managerial personnel by training more capable individuals for managerial positions is handicapped by the continuing requirement that, as Novotny phrased it in his last New Year's message, "capable and *politically conscious* individuals be appointed to leading posts."[49] Nevertheless, the trend appears to be in the direction of greater emphasis on qualifications and less emphasis on "political maturity."[50]

All this is not to say that the outlook for the New Economic Model is altogether bleak; with time many of the present difficulties could be overcome. The big question is whether the party leaders who still hold the reins of power will be willing to relax their grip sufficiently to permit the advantages of the proposed reforms to take full effect. Yet, whether it likes the new course or not, the regime itself is in large measure dependent on the reforms' success. The only alternative is a regression to the old system of management, which has proven inadequate, and further economic failures, which even a totalitarian Communist government can politically ill afford in Eastern Europe today. . . .

[49] *Ceteka,* Jan. 1, 1965. Emphasis mine.

[50] A party Central Committee resolution passed at the January 1965 Plenum provided that less capable individuals must not be given priority because of their party affiliation. (*Rude pravo,* Feb. 4, 1965.) The fact that such a resolution was passed is indicative of how matters of this nature must have been handled in the past.

On March 16, 1965, Radio Prague announced the establishment of a statewide commission to study the means for raising the professional qualifications of leading economic executives. In the same broadcast, it was pointed out that in Poland and Yugoslavia the percentage of factory managers with a university education is three times as high as in Czechoslovakia, and that in United States plants with more than 500 employees it is seven times as high (78 per cent).

PART THREE

PRICES, PROFITS, AND PLANNING

INTRODUCTION

Ever since the Russians initiated the Five Year Plans in 1928, they have been searching for measures to evaluate the efficiency of enterprises. Having attacked production for profit rather than for use, it was not easy for Communists, once in power, to adopt the old capitalist criterion and goal of maximizing profits for each firm. Output and input norms, quotas, and a host of supplementary criteria for measuring success were developed. As the economy grew in complexity and size so did the success criteria. The shortcomings of these criteria had been discussed extensively outside of the Communist world.[1] Within the Communist countries, however, even where economists considered the price mechanism far superior to physical controls for allocating resources efficiently—as in Poland—the issue was slow to see the light of day or to have much influence at the policy level.

During the last few years, prompted by academicians like Kantarovich,[2] V. S. Nemchinov,[3] and Yevsei Liberman, the debate has grown in intensity and openness. In its frankest and least ideological form, it still appears more strongly outside of the Soviet Union.

The debate has also led to some cautious experiments with the use of profits as a measure of efficiency and with consumer demand rather than the commands of the planning hierarchies guiding the production of some enterprises.

[1] For a classic discussion of these criteria see Alec Nove, "The Problem of Success Indicators in Soviet Industry," *Economica*, Feb. 1958, pp. 1–13.

[2] Benjamin Ward, "Kantarovich on Economic Calculation," *Journal of Political Economy*, Dec. 1960, pp. 545–556.

[3] See for example his "Socialist Management and Production Planning," *Kommunist*, 1964, 5; translated in *Problems of Economics*, July 1965, pp. 21–32.

Professor Liberman, who is credited with much of the new look in Soviet economics, promptly set about refuting the argument that these new developments augur a return to capitalism in *Soviet Life*. The function of profits, Liberman argues, is different in a planned "socialist" (Communist) economy than under capitalism. It is simply a measure of efficiency, the surplus of sales over costs, in "socialism" (the term used by Marxists to describe present-day transitional societies supposedly moving towards communism under their direction). Besides, under "socialism," reasons Liberman, profits are obtained not by manipulating prices and other monopolistic practices, but by cutting costs. Liberman, however, is not willing to go so far as to make profits the measure of efficiency. He wants the composition of output to be governed by the composition of demand. This he believes is compatible with the planning of aggregate consumer demand.

Indeed, he goes further and asserts, "Centralized planning is wholly compatible with the initiative of enterprises"—a judgment not fully shared, in the sense Liberman uses the term central planning, by such eminent Polish Marxists as Oskar Lange[4] and Josef Pajestka,[5] Czech economist, Klas, and his own countrymen, V. Belkin, and I. Birman.

Belkin and Birman advocate the use of profits as the main index of efficiency. They realize the revolutionary nature of their advocacy, to wit: "Profit will be able to play its role as the main index only if the costs and results of production are correctly estimated." They go on to establish the need for charging interest on capital so as to reckon costs properly and for pricing all goods correctly. However, they do not tell us how these correct prices are to be estimated and by whom. "The unsatisfactory condition of prices has been noted by all the recent party Congresses and Central Committee plenary meetings. It is time to ask why the party decisions have not been fulfilled, why public opinion is being ignored." The questions are intriguing. Who is ignoring "the party decisions"? The planners? the ministers? the managers? Who indeed has the power to ignore the party and

[4] Oskar Lange, *The Political Economy of Socialism* (Van Keulen, The Hague, 1958), pp. 16–28.

[5] Josef Pajestka, "Changes in Planning and Management," *Polish Perspectives*, April 1965, pp. 15–20. Also see L. Kolodziejezyk, "Rentability and Profit," *Polish Perspectives*, June 1965, pp. 54–56.

the public? Or is it that public opinion does not count, and the party is too confused to determine "correct" prices while the bureaucracy finds it easier to live with the status quo than to change it?

Liberman is quite revolutionary in criticizing a long-standing Soviet orthodoxy which considers the law of value "as an unpleasant leftover from capitalism." But he too does not quite spell out his thoughts on the appropriate mechanism for price formation.

Belkin and Birman agree with Liberman that the use of profit as an index would not make a communist economy over into capitalism because "the evil of capitalism lies not in its drive for profit, but in its distribution in the obtaining of income not in accordance with work performed but in accordance with the amount of capital owned." In a more ideological tone, Liberman asserts, "Under capitalism, profit is the goal, and the satisfaction of the needs of the population is the means. Under socialism it is just the other way around." A critic of both systems may be reminded of the Polish wag, who is reported to have said, "Under capitalism man exploits man; under socialism it is just the reverse." An American critic of Soviet "socialism" could point out that in the U.S. all the plant equipment and the profits from these belong to the bosses, but the cars jamming the parking lots outside factory gates belong to the workers while in the U.S.S.R. the factories and equipment and profits all belong to the workers but the few cars in the parking lot belong to the bosses.

There is not much discussion of the desirability of recreating a full-blown market mechanism in the Soviet Union. Without some efficient mechanism for the estimation of correct (equilibrium) prices, decentralization could not go very far in improving the efficiency of a planned economy. If prices are to be used as primary signals for guiding the output plans and input choices of firms, these could only lead to wrong decisions as long as the prices are incorrect. Mathematical economists, who realize this most acutely have, perhaps for this reason, been comparatively quiet in this current debate.[6] However, mathematical economics, after having been treated for years as a symptom of bourgois decadence, has become very respectable in

[6] Robert W. Campbell, "Economics: Roads and Inroads," *Problems of Communism*, Nov.-Dec. 1965, pp. 23–33.

recent years.[7] The substitution of input-output tables for "material balances" necessitates planning in value terms. The persistence of incorrect values can, therefore, only impede the most effective utilization of the new tools of this science and of computers for purposes of planning.

Leon Smolinski reviews the evolution of economic planning in the Soviet Union and discusses the prospects and directions of probable change. Use of correct prices, of mathematical tools and of computers is likely to make the economy much more efficient, and as in American industry, may promote centralization rather than decentralization. After all, the perfect computer with the perfect plan is a perfect substitute for perfect competition. In real life, as has been pointed out by Peter Wiles,[8] the choice is between imperfect computation and imperfect competition.

It is not inconceivable that Soviet planning may turn toward more competition and less computation. If it does, it would not necessarily be a cause for celebration by supporters of capitalism, for as Smolinski points out: "rationally allocated resources may serve highly irrational ends. Indeed, to the extent we mistrust the Soviet ends, it might be 'rational' on our part to root for the all-out centralizers ridiculed by Birman. Their attempts to plan everything would soon turn everyone into a planner. And an economy á la Glushkov where everyone is engaged in paperwork may not be efficient but is, at least, likely to be peaceful."

[7] Wassily Leontief, "The Decline and Rise of Soviet Economic Science," *Foreign Affairs,* Jan. 1960, pp. 261–272; also Robert W. Campbell, "Marx, Kantarovich and Novozhilov: Stoimost' versus Reality," *Slavic Review,* Oct. 1961, pp. 402–418.

[8] Peter Wiles, "Imperfect Competition and Decentralized Planning," *Economies of Planning,* vol. 4, No. 1, 1964, pp. 16–28.

YEVSEI LIBERMAN

Are We Flirting with Capitalism?
Profits and "Profits"*

In its February 12 issue this year *Time* magazine carried my picture on its cover, with the prominent caption, "The Communist Flirtation with Profits." The cover story, entitled "Borrowing from the Capitalists," made many references to my writings and statements, and drew conclusions vastly different from those I make. I therefore asked the editors of *Soviet Life* and *Ekonomicheskaya Gazeta* to permit me to comment on the *Time* article in their publications. To do a proper job, I shall have to go rather deeply into the essential character of profits.

Profits are the monetary form of the surplus product, that is, the product which working people produce over and above their personal needs. The surplus product is, therefore, an expression of the productivity of labor. Primitive man ate or used up what he produced. As civilization and technology progressed, labor began to create not only the equivalent of the working people's means of subsistence but something more. This something more was the surplus product, the very same surplus product that supports the entire nonproductive sphere, from the watchman to the banker and cabinet minister.

But the surplus product is also the source of means essential for the development of society. That applied to feudal and capitalist society, and it applies to socialism and communism.

Under socialism products and services are also produced as commodities and also sold chiefly for money. Therefore, the surplus product inevitably assumes the monetary form of profits. But since profits in our country are used in the interests of society, they become less and less an expression of surplus (unpaid) labor and come more and more to express socially necessary labor.

What is the difference between capitalist and socialist profits?

* Reprinted from *Soviet Life,* July 1965.

BONUS "FOR RISKS"

The difference is not, of course, that private enterprise stands for profit while socialism "denounces" it, as economists in the West often claim. To make the difference clear, let us examine 1) how profit is formed, 2) what it signifies, and 3) for what purposes it is spent.

From the private entrepreneur's viewpoint, all profit belongs to the capitalist. To support this view, economists built the theory of the three factors that create value: capital, land and labor. In *The Theory of Economic Development* Joseph A. Schumpeter says that profit is everything above cost. But this "cost" includes "wages" for the labor of the entrepreneur, land rent, interest on capital, as well as a bonus "for risks." On top of that, the entrepreneur reaps a profit if he succeeds, by a new combination of production elements, in reducing the cost to below the existing price level.

What kind of "combination of elements" this is can be seen from the fact that the main part of the profit under the private enterprise system now comes not so much from production as from the process of exchange. For instance, high profits come most readily from advantageous buying of raw materials, the raising of retail prices, the tendency of unemployment to lower wages, nonequivalent exchange with developing countries, the export of capital to countries where wages are low, the system of preferential tariffs and customs duties, raising the prices of stocks on the stock exchange, and so-called *Grunder* (speculator's) profits.

DOES MONEY SMELL IN THE SOVIET UNION?

All those sources of profit are ruled out in the Soviet Union owing to the very nature of socialism, under which there is neither private ownership of the means of production nor stock capital and, consequently, no stock market. The level of payment for labor depends on its productivity and is regulated by law. The prices of raw and other materials are planned; market conditions that could be taken advantage of in purchasing raw materials or hiring labor do not exist. Nor can the prices of finished articles be raised by taking advantage of market conditions. Exchange with other countries is conducted on the basis of equality and long-term agreements.

Legend has it that the Roman Emperor Vespasian decided to impose a tax on public toilets when he saw that his treasury was running law. His son Titus, who later succeeded to the throne, waxed indignant at such an evil-smelling source of revenue. Vespasian then held up to his son's nose the first receipts from the toilet tax. *"Non olet!"* ("It doesn't smell!") Titus exclaimed in surprise. Ever since then the view that "money doesn't smell" has been gospel in the commodity world. Indeed, under private enterprise nobody really cares how money is made. The important thing is to make it, the important thing is how much of it you can make.

But in the Soviet Union "money does smell." That will be seen if we look into the nature of profit. In our country profit testifies, in principle, only to the level of production efficiency. Profit is the difference between the selling price of articles and their cost. But since our prices, in principle, express the norms of expenditure of socially necessary labor, the difference is an indicator of the comparative economy with which an item is produced. Behind Soviet profits there is nothing except hours of working time, tons of raw and other materials and fuel, and kilowatt-hours of electrical energy that have been saved. Our profits cannot "smell" of anything but that. We do not justify profits obtained through accidental circumstances — for example, excessive prices — and we do not consider such profit a credit to the factory or other enterprise which makes it. We look on such profits, rather, as the result of an insufficiently flexible practice of price fixing. All such profits go into the state budget, without any bonus to the enterprise concerned.

Capitalist profit is a different matter altogether. As the reader knows very well, profits in the West can indicate anything under the sun over and above purely technical and organizational efficiency. Commercial dexterity, successful advertising, profitable orders for military production — that is what the history of present-day big capital testifies to sooner than to anything else. Surely it must be clear that in essence and origin profit under socialism bears only a superficial resemblance to profit under private enterprise, while by its nature and by the factors to which it testifies it is fundamentally different from capitalist profit.

Where do profits go in the Soviet Union? First of all, neither a single individual nor a single enterprise can appropriate profits. Profits are not arbitrarily invested by any persons or groups for the sake of private income.

Profits belong to those to whom the means of production belong, that is, to all citizens, to society. Profits go, first and foremost, for the planned expansion and improvement of production and scientific research, and to provide free social services for the people: education, health, pensions, scholarships. Part is spent on the management apparatus and, unfortunately, a rather large part goes for defense needs. We would gladly give up this last expenditure if a program of general disarmament were adopted.

INDICATORS IN INDUSTRY

There is nothing new in that use of profits in the Soviet Union. Our enterprises have been making profits in money form for more than 40 years, ever since 1921. It is with these profits that we have built up our giant industrial potential, thanks to which we have moved to a leading position in world science and technology. And we have accomplished this without major long-term credits from other countries.

Why has the question of profits been so widely discussed in the Soviet Union lately? Not because profits did not exist before and are only now being introduced. *The reason is that profit was not, and still is not, used as the major over-all indicator of the efficient operation of our enterprises.* Besides profit, we have been using a fairly large number of obligatory indicators — among others, gross output, assortment, lower costs, number of employees, size of payroll, output per employee, and average wages. The multiplicity of indicators hamstrung the initiative of the enterprises. Their main concern often was to turn out as great a volume of goods as possible since they would be rated chiefly on gross output. Furthermore, enterprises did not pay much attention to how they used their assets. Trying to meet their output quotas in the easiest way for themselves, they asked for, and received free from the state, a great deal of plant, which they did not always use efficiently or to full capacity.

How do we explain that?

VIRTUE BECOMES VICE

For a long time the Soviet Union was the only socialist country. We stood alone, surrounded by a world in which there were many who wanted to change our social system by force. We had to build up our own industries and secure our defenses at all costs and in the shortest possible time. Such considerations as the quality and appearance of goods, or even their cost, did not count. This policy completely justified itself. The Soviet Union not only held its own in the war of 1941–1945 but played the decisive role in saving the world from fascism. That was worth any price. And that was our "profit" then.

But, as Lenin often said, our virtues, if exaggerated, can turn into vices. And that is what happened when we held to the same administrative methods of economic management after we entered the stage of peaceful economic competition with the industrial countries of the West.

We want to give every citizen, not only the well-to-do, a high standard of living, in the intellectual as well as in the material sense. In other words, we want everyone to have the fullest opportunity to develop his mental and physical capacities and his individual (I emphasize, individual, and not group) inclinations and interests. We want every person in our country to be able to do the work he wants most to do. We want to reach the point where it will not be possible to draw a hard and fast line between a person's vocation and his avocation.

Before we can bring people's intellectual capacities to full flower, we must satisfy their material needs, place goods and services of high quality within everyone's reach. These needs must be satisfied, moreover, with the lowest possible production outlays and the fullest possible utilization of all assets.

WHAT IS THE WAY OUT?

All that cannot be done through the old methods of administrative direction and highly centralized management. We must change over to a system whereby the enterprises themselves have a material incentive to provide the best possible service to the consumer. It is clear that to do this we must free the enterprises from the excessive number of obligatory indicators. In my opinion, the criteria for rating the work of enterprises should be: *first,* how well they carry out their plans of deliveries (in actual products); and, if these plans are fulfilled, then *second,* their level of profitability. I believe that out of their profits, enterprises should have to pay into the state budget a certain percentage of the value of their assets as "payment for use of plant." The purpose would be to spur enterprises to make the most productive use of their assets. Part of the remaining share of the profits would go into incentive pay system funds, the amount depending on the level of profitability. The rest of the profits would accrue to the state budget to finance the expansion of production and to satisfy the welfare needs of the population.

PLAN, PROFIT AND BONUS

Why do I choose profit as the indicator? Because profit generalizes all aspects of operation, including quality of output. The prices of better articles have to be correspondingly higher than those of articles that are outmoded and not properly suited to their purpose. It is important to note, however, that profit in this case is neither the sole nor the chief aim of production. We are interested above all in products with which to meet the needs of the people and of industry. Profit is used merely as the main generalizing and stimulating indicator of efficiency, as a device for rating the operation of enterprises.

Yet Western press comments on my writings blare away about the term "profit," very often ignoring the fact that the title of my *Pravda* article of September 9, 1962, was "The Plan, Profits and Bonuses." They make a lot of noise about profit but say nothing about planning.

Actually, my point is to encourage enterprises, by means of bonuses from profits, to draw up good plans, that is, plans which are advantageous both to themselves and to society. And not only to draw them up but carry them out, with encouragement from profits. It is not a question of relaxing (or rejecting) planning but, on the contrary, of improving it by drawing the enterprises themselves, first and foremost, into the planning process, for the enterprises always know their real potentialities best and should study and know the demands of their customers.

The contractual relations with consumers or customers that we are now starting to introduce in several branches of light industry by no means signify that we are going over to regulation by the market. We have better ways of predicting consumer demand because we know the wage fund of the urban population and the incomes of the collective farmers. Therefore, we can draw up scientific patterns of the population's income and expenditure. In our country consumer demand, in terms of total volume, is a factor that lends itself to planning. However, the various elements of that volume — for instance, the colors of sweaters or the styles of suits factories should produce, or how best to organize their production — need not be the prerogatives of centralized planning but matters on which the stores and the factories concerned come to terms. Thus, the consideration of consumer demand and the planning of production are not only compatible in the Soviet Union but can strongly substantiate and supplement each other.

THE SUBSTANCE OF OUR DEBATES

The *Time* cover story is full of contradictions. It admits that the Soviet people now have more money and that there is a growing demand for better and more fashionable clothing and for private cars. One would think that pointed to an improving economy, yet the article claims that the switch to profits is a result of "unsettling prospects," of "waste, mismanagement, inefficiency and planning gone berserk," and so on and so forth.

There are, of course, no few instances of waste and mismanagement in the Soviet economy, just as there are in private enterprise; think of the thousands of firms that go bankrupt every year. But in the Soviet Union we focus public attention on instances of waste and mismanagement. We publicize and criticize them openly. Some Western commentators take advantage of that fact. What better way can there be of distorting an over-all picture than to pick haphazard details and offer them as representative of the whole? The over-all picture shows that the Soviet Union increased its output by 7.1 per cent in 1964. *Time* admits that this is a very good growth rate for a highly developed economy. It is not good enough for us, however. We are used to growth rates expressed in two digits. *Time* does not mention that the reason for this 7.1 per cent growth rate, a relatively modest one for us, was the 1963 crop failure.

We are turning to profits not because we need a "sheet anchor." We are not in any danger. The fact remains, however, that we have to improve our methods of economic management. This is the substance of our debates and our searches.

THE MAIN FUNCTION OF PROFITS

Under socialism, profits can be a yardstick of production efficiency to a far greater degree than in the West, for in the Soviet Union profits follow, in principle, only from technological and organizational improvement. This also means that profits here will play an important but subsidiary role, like money in general, not the main role. After providing a yardstick of production achievement and a means of encouraging such achievement, profits in the Soviet Union are used wholly for the needs of society. They are returned to the population in the form of social services and expanded production, which guarantees full employment and better and easier working conditions for everyone.

In the Soviet Union nobody accumulates profits in money form — neither the state nor enterprises. This is an important point to grasp. If, for instance, at the end of the year the state as a whole has a surplus of budget revenue over expenditure, the surplus does not stay in the form of accumulated currency but is immediately used for two purposes: 1) to increase State Bank credits for material stocks, in other words, the surplus takes the material form of expanding inventories in production or trade, while money only measures this increase, and 2) to withdraw paper money from circulation, that is, to increase the purchasing power of the ruble on the free collective farm markets, where prices are determined by supply and demand.

Consequently, profits cannot become either capital or hoarded treasure in the Soviet Union. They are not, therefore, a social goal or a motive force in production as a whole. The motive force in production under socialism is the satisfaction of the steadily growing material and cultural needs of the population. However, profit can be, and should be, an indicator (and the key indicator, moreover) of production efficiency. It should serve to encourage workers to raise their efficiency. But it should be understood that encouragement from profits is not distribution of the results of production on the basis of capital. Distribution is still on the basis of work; it is work that rules distribution under socialism.

THE GOAL AND THE MEANS

The significance of profit in the Soviet Union was underestimated owing to a certain disregard of the law of value. Some Soviet economists incorrectly interpreted that law as an unpleasant leftover from capitalism and said we had to get rid of it as quickly as possible. Shelving the law of value led to arbitrary fixing of planned prices and to prices that operated over too long a period. As a result, prices became divorced from the real value of goods, while profits fluctuated greatly from enterprise to enterprise, even on comparable articles. Under those conditions profits were poor reflections of the actual achievements in production. Because of this, many economists and economic managers began to consider profit as something completely independent of production and, hence, as a poor guide in matters of economic management. This is the delusion many Soviet economists, among them the present author, are now trying to expose. We do not intend to go back to private enterprise but, on the contrary, to permit the economic laws of socialism to operate. Centralized planning is wholly compatible with the initiative of enterprises. This is as far from private enterprise as private enterprise is from feudalism.

The law of value is not a law of capitalism but a law of all commodity production, including planned commodity production under socialism. The difference from capitalism is that the goal and the means have changed places. Under capitalism, profit is the goal, and the satisfaction of the needs of the population is the means. Under socialism it is just the other way around. Satisfaction of the needs of the population is the goal, and profit is the means. The difference is not one of terms but of substance.

"TIME" AND THE SOVIET ECONOMY

Soviet economists can only smile when they read how *Time* interprets the socialist planning system. It says: "A knitwear plant ordered to produce 80,000 caps and sweaters naturally produced only caps: they were smaller and thus cheaper and quicker to make." In other words, the factory had freedom of choice. But elsewhere the same article says that factories are tied hand and foot by the plan, and that the plans account for each nail and electric bulb. Where is the logic?

Another example: "Taxi drivers were put on a bonus system based on mileage, and soon the Moscow suburbs were full of empty taxis barreling down the boulevards to fatten their bonuses." But every Moscow schoolboy knows that the bonus of taxi drivers is based on the amount they collect in fares. Empty runs are a disadvantage. As a matter of fact, there is a restriction on the mileage of empty runs. Taxis in Moscow and many other cities are radio dispatched, the purpose being to reduce empty runs. Such lack of knowledge on the part of the *Time* staff can hardly make for an objective appraisal of the Soviet economy.

The magazine's statement on more serious matters are just as informed. Experimental garment factories, it says, "showed such a resounding improvement in efficiency — and such 'deviationism' — that many Kremlinologists assumed they had contributed to Nikita's downfall."

In the first place, these factories did not show any "resounding" improvement in efficiency. On the contrary, their output dropped owing to a greater outlay of labor for more painstaking manufacture and finishing of the articles. The only thing they showed is that when given the right to plan their output on the basis of orders from stores, they can make good suits of wool and man-made fiber mixtures at a lower price. Customers readily buy these suits.

In the second place, what kind of "deviationism" is it if the "deviation" was made in conformity with instructions issued by the Economic Council of the USSR in March 1964 — without any direct participation by Professor Liberman, whom the Western press cites, without having sufficient grounds for doing so, on every occasion when steps are taken to improve the Soviet economy. My modest role, like that of many other of our economists, is to study methods of improving economic management on the basis of the principles and economic laws of socialism.

RIVERS DON'T FLOW BACKWARD

Soviet economists have no intention of testing the economic methods of private enterprise. We expect to get along with our own methods, sharpening the tried and tested instrument of material incentive on the grindstone of profit. This has been one of our instruments for a long time, but it has grown dull, chiefly because we didn't use it enough. Now we are sharpening it and it will, we hope, serve socialism well. But this does not mean that we are either giving up a planned economy or turning toward the system of private enterprise. Rivers do not flow backward. And if, at high water, rivers make turns, they are simply cutting better and shorter channels for themselves. They are not looking for a way to go back.

V. BELKIN AND I. BIRMAN

Independence of the Enterprise and Economic Stimuli*

Many of the economy's executives have high hopes for the statute on the enterprise and are waiting for this important document to appear.

In our view, the chief element in the statute should be the consistent realization of the universally recognized method of organizing and managing the enterprise — cost accounting, a method that

* From V. Belkin and I. Birman, "Independence of the Enterprise and Economic Stimuli," *Problems of Economics,* Vol. VIII, No. 3 (July 1965), pp. 37–40. Reprinted by permission of International Arts and Sciences Press.

is expected to ensure an organic combination of the interests of the state with those of the enterprise and individual workers.

Since the introduction of cost accounting, production has grown tremendously and the complexity of centralized planning and management has increased even more. True, our enterprises are now managed by experienced specialists, the cultural and technical level has increased, and the activity of the workers, engineers and office employees has intensified. It appeared that these factors required an expansion and strengthening of the economic independence of the enterprise. Of course, the economies of the regions continued to develop, but a cumbersome system of petty tutelage of the enterprise took firm root at the same time.

Yet the very concept of "cost accounting" implies that the enterprise itself should determine how to achieve the best results. But other agencies — the economic councils, branch committees and planning bodies — do this job for it. And it is established practice to criticize these bodies for unsatisfactory planning and management of the enterprises. It is high time to realize that guidance of the enterprises by means of administrative intervention in all the details is a very poor method that cannot yield good results.

There are people who believe that it will be possible to achieve completely centralized management of the economy with the help of computing techniques. This is an illusion.

The main line of work of the authors of this article is employment of electronic computers in the economy. We would very much like to see clever machines display their capabilities in this field too. But no matter how advanced electronic computers may become, a system under which everything — to the very last bolt — is planned and managed from a single center is an impossibility.

Moreover, electronic computers have hardly benefited economic planning and management as yet, mainly because current practices in economic management are not adapted to working out and, above all, executing optimum solutions.

Here is a case in point. It is now clear that the elaboration of optimum schemes for goods shipments yields a sizable saving. This is not a complicated task. It has been the subject of many articles and books, and not a few dissertations on the question have been defended. Yet there are hardly any shipments made under optimum schemes. Why not? Precisely because the transport agencies, contrary to common sense, are given plans expressed in ton-kilometers, and optimum schemes reduce the number of ton-kilometers. It is possible to set up all sorts of computing centers, to devise superb algorithms, but there will be no progress as long as the transport agencies are held accountable under the plan in ton-kilometers.

Since the question of computing techniques has been raised, it should be pointed out that the crux of the problem of introducing electronic computers involves economic preconditions — the need to reconstruct the system of planning and management and to create economic stimuli that will operate in the right direction. Only under these conditions will electronic computing techniques be able to produce (and will produce) a tremendous effect. Only then will a unified network of computing centers serve a useful purpose.

The methods of managing the economy should be economic in nature. We must devise a system in which the material interests of the enterprise as a whole and of each individual worker are served by the maximum utilization of reserves and potentialities, a system in which these interests will fully coincide with those of the state. What is good for society should be beneficial for each individual worker.

The existing practice in planning, calculating, and evaluating the results of the work of the enterprise satisfies this natural requirement only to a small extent. The fact that the interests of the enterprise and of society fail to coincide is an artificial condition which results from the work of the enterprise being appraised in accordance with the degree of fulfillment of numerous excessively minute and detailed plan assignments. When the work of the enterprise is evaluated according to the degree of fulfillment of the plan and planning is conducted on the basis of the level achieved, the enterprise is impelled to conceal its reserves and to ask for lower plan targets.

It follows that the work of the enterprise should be appraised not in accordance with numerous indices that are incomparable, disconnected, and often contradictory, but in accordance with one major index of a general character that will best reflect the result of the effort of the enterprise's personnel and management.

There is no need to invent such an index. It follows from the very essence of cost accounting, which consists in comparing and collating the results of production with the costs, in having the results not only fully cover the costs, but exceed them as much as possible. The difference between the results and costs is profit. The greater the profit, the better the work of the enterprise. Therefore, it is necessary to encourage and stimulate the obtaining of profit.

Nor is there any need to invent economic stimuli. They already exist in the form of bonuses. Therefore, bonuses and other incentives should be strictly dependent on the size of the profit derived.

The introduction of profit as the main index will also make it possible objectively to appraise the work of the apparatus of economic management. The size of the profit derived by the enterprises under the given management agency will help determine whether the personnel of that agency have worked well. Each executive will be appraised objectively and accurately.

Those who are against making profit the main index hypocritically allude to the capitalist system. But the evil of capitalism lies not in the drive for profit, but in its distribution, in the obtaining of income not in accordance with work performed but in accordance with the amount of capital owned. In our case, the effort to obtain profit will result in the creation of greater real benefits, in better satisfaction of the requirements of the working people.

Profit will be able to play its role as the main index only if the costs and results of production are correctly estimated. Today the costs are not reckoned adequately; fixed assets are not fully reflected in them and circulating assets are not reflected at all. Society presents the fixed and circulating assets to the enterprise without charge. True, there are amortization charges on the fixed assets, although there is no such charge on circulating assets. But amortization is actually reimbursement of the value of the fixed assets, and the enterprise does not pay anything for the use of the fixed assets. When an enterprise takes money from a bank on credit, it not only returns the money, but also pays a certain amount of interest for the use of the money. Then why does not the enterprise pay anything for the use of the fixed and circulating assets? Since these assets are granted without charge, the enterprise does not try to make the best possible use of them.

It has been estimated, with the help of electronic computers, that one ruble invested in the expansion of fixed assets or material circulating assets now saves 15 kopecks of current outlays each year. It follows that if an enterprise fails to utilize its fixed assets or has superfluous circulating assets, it burdens the state with an annual loss of 15% of their value. It is essential economically to stimulate the most efficient use of fixed and circulating assets. And the best way to do this is to impose a special charge for the use of these assets.

The profitability index of an enterprise should be expressed in the size of the profit as related to the value of the fixed and circulating assets at its disposal.

Prices should also be worked out so that they incorporate the cost of production and a percentage of the value of the fixed and circulating assets. The existing prices do not comply with this principle, and their deviation from actual expenditures causes undesirable phenomena. Incorrect prices, for instance, constitute one of the main reasons why our economists overlooked the advantages inherent in the accelerated development of the chemical industry.

Estimates reveal that wholesale prices deviate substantially from actual costs, and in different degrees. For instance, the level of prices on fuel and power is 1.4 times below the prices on machine-building products, and the latter, in turn, are 1.6 times below those on items produced by the light and food industries. Given such differences in price levels, the enterprise is not in a position to use them as levers to secure solutions that will be advantageous to society as a whole.

And it is not only the enterprises, but also the planning bodies that find it difficult to operate without economically substantiated prices. In order to determine whether one or another branch of industry is progressive, our economists often have to look across the ocean, and this should not be the only guide for them.

Our economists have long argued this question. More and more research workers and executives have been coming out in favor of prices that correspond to the actual costs of production. But those people in our state who are responsible for this important work pretend that this is not their concern at all. They approach the question of prices not from the standpoint of the interests of production, but from a primitively conceived financial point of view. One cannot help recalling "primitive mercantilists" in this connection. The unsatisfactory condition of prices has been noted by all the recent party congresses and Central Committee plenary meetings. It is time to ask why the party decisions have not been fulfilled, why public opinion is being ignored.

Extension of the independence of the enterprise and reinforcement of the role of economic stimuli do not mean that planning will be abolished or replaced. It goes without saying that the state will continue to effectuate a policy of planned capital investments.

The proposed measures should not be regarded as a single and final solution of all questions. The point of issue is only the creation of the foundation for further transformations, which should be introduced gradually after thorough preparation.

We believe that it would be advisable gradually to abolish control over the number of people to be employed and the wage fund. It is necessary to increase the norms of amortization, having included in them compensation for obsolescence. The enterprises should be given the right to amend the output plan with the consent of the customer. The plan should be based on orders from the customers.

It might be advisable, in establishing planned prices, to regard the prices as maximum prices which cannot be exceeded and to permit products to be sold at prices below those fixed. On the other hand, when an enterprise is producing a product of the best quality or a product with higher consumer properties than are stipulated by the standards, it should be given the right to fix the price with the agreement of the customer.

Substantial changes are also necessary in the field of construction. Construction organizations should not be financed on the basis of the volume of construction and assembly work actually performed, as is now the practice, but should be granted credits and payment only for completed projects that have been commissioned. And the rate of interest on the credit should be sufficiently high. If this is done the builders will not scatter funds over a large number of projects; they will be economically, that is, more effectively, encouraged to commission the projects as rapidly as possible.

The urgent need to introduce fundamental improvements into our methods of economic management is obvious. Open the latest statistical yearbook issued by the Central Statistical Administration and you will see that the effectiveness of capital investments in the national economy has dropped in recent years. One can easily imagine the losses incurred by the national economy as a result of this tendency. This is the price we pay for deferring the solution of questions that became urgent long ago.

It follows from the above that the question of the economic statute on the enterprise is by no means of local importance. To adopt the statute will mean to carry out a series of essential measures. This is completely possible and advisable, for these measures will bring our national economy incalculable benefits.

LEON SMOLINSKI

What Next in
Soviet Planning?*

ACADEMICIAN Victor Glushkov, the head of the Soviet program of research in cybernetics, estimated recently that, failing a radical reform in planning methods, the planning bureaucracy would grow 36-fold by 1980, requiring the services of the entire Soviet population. Such warnings are not exactly novel. Some forty years ago, the dying Lenin wrote: "Vital work we do is sinking in a dead sea of paperwork. We get sucked in by a foul bureaucratic swamp." In 1933, Leon Trotsky saw acute symptoms of the same disease. "Bureaucracy acts at random," he wrote, "it rejects objective criteria, it does not recognize laws other than the law of its own will, it substitutes commands for plans and pressure for calculation."[1]

Trotsky's indictment reads surprisingly like Premier Khrushchev's recent attacks upon Gosplan and its methods. The disease he recognized has now reached an acute stage and may seriously impede further growth of the Soviet economy. Until recently, analysis of these important processes was difficult because of the lack of information. In particular, little was known about the way in which economic decisions are actually made at the top and at the enterprise level. Interesting disclosures made recently about these previously forbidden matters have not yet received the attention they deserve.

II

A centrally planned economy is usually looked upon as a more or less efficient machine for the production and distribution of goods. A cybernetician would view it somewhat differently: as a machine which, more or less efficiently, generates, processes and distributes information. The two functions are intimately related. Channels of information and flows of commodities are, in fact, interrelated parts of a highly complex network. To produce a carload of, say, ball

* From Leon Smolinski, "What Next in Soviet Planning?" *Foreign Affairs* (July 1964), pp. 602–613. Reprinted by permission of *Foreign Affairs*. Copyright by the Council on Foreign Relations, Inc., New York.

[1] *Biulleten' opozitsii*, 1933, No. 33, p. 2.

bearings, it takes not only so much steel, machinery, manpower and time; it also takes an information input in the form of data concerning the availability of resources and the demand for the product. These data are gathered, processed and forwarded to the decision-makers who issue orders to producers and receive reports which may give rise to new, modified decisions.

All these activities can obviously be handled in a variety of ways. The flow of information may take place within the confines of a small privately owned shop or, at the other extreme, it may involve thousands of messages passing among hundreds of agencies. Whatever the nature of the information system involved, a cybernetician would begin his analysis with such questions as: How much information is needed per unit of output (say, per carload of ball bearings), and what is its cost? Who receives the data and in what detail? Who processes them and by what means? Who makes the decisions? How is their execution controlled?

To provide satisfactory answers to these questions in the Soviet case and to follow our carload of ball bearings through all the recesses of the information system, nothing short of a treatise on the organization and functioning of the Soviet economy would do. Significantly enough, such a treatise would also go a long way toward answering the question how Russia is ruled. Information flows point toward centers of power. "Knowledge is power," asserted Francis Bacon.

But power wielded is not necessarily in proportion to the knowledge possessed. An acute disproportion of this kind seems to lie at the heart of Soviet planners' present difficulties. The Stalinist solution to economic planning and administration which still survives in the Soviet Union amounts to highly centralized, authoritarian decision-making, based on inadequate information and imposed upon the enterprises by long chains of bureaucratic command. To the extent that up-to-date, well-coordinated information is lacking, decisions — including some key choices which affect the course of economic development for years to come — tend to be based on rules of thumb and intuition. But intuition is a poor substitute for information in directing a complex, modern economy. Uninformed choices are costly and wasteful. The famous mathematician, L. V. Kantorovich, estimates that the introduction of more rational methods of economic planning and administration would raise Soviet industrial output by as much as 50 per cent without additional inputs.

In the Soviet economy central planners decide by-and-large not only what but also how to produce. In this system, an enterprise, throughout its life cycle, is essentially a recipient of commands and a supplier of data on which subsequent commands are in turn based.

Let us examine first the birth permit of a Soviet enterprise, its so-called *proiekt*. Central planners have a virtual monopoly of investment decisions. Through the annual investment plan they apportion funds among industries and, within an industry, among individual projects. No industrial establishment may be legally built without a detailed *proiekt, viz.* engineering design, cost estimates and blueprints, prepared by a central designing organization according to the planners' directives, approved by the latter and then transmitted to the builders for execution.

One is immediately impressed by the extraordinary amount of detailed information reported to the planners and sent out by them as orders in connection with these decisions. The project of the Novo Lipetsk steel mill, for example, comprises 91 volumes totaling 70,000 pages (one is not surprised to learn that the designers are paid by the sheet . . .). "Literally everything is anticipated in these blueprints, the emplacement of each nail, lamp or washstand. Only one aspect of the project is not considered at all: its economic effectiveness."[2] In fact, the actual cost of building a factory is difficult and often impossible to establish. "Nor is anyone really interested in it." The same is true of projects for new machinery.[3]

Thus, paradoxically enough, while the planners receive and send out literally carloads of engineering data in connection with each important investment decision, they remain ignorant of perhaps the most crucial implications of their choices — the project's economic effectiveness and the cost of the alternatives foregone.

The basic operational directive which is to guide the Soviet factory manager in his day-by-day activities is his annual *Tekhpromfinplan*. This voluminous document sets out for each year in advance the volume and assortment of output, the methods of production to be employed, the cost and physical amount of each input to be used, the financial results (profits, cost reduction, etc.) to be aimed at in each quarter and month, and much more.

Preparation of that document is both time- and labor-consuming. It takes more than six months to complete the job. And then, as was recently disclosed, a curious thing happens. "This most important planning document does not perform the role assigned to it. Instead of serving the purposes of the day-by-day operational guidance, it is filed away in the factory's archives and in the Sovnarkhoz's archives and is consulted only in extreme cases."[4]

[2] *Izvestia,* April 20, 1963; *Ekonomicheskaia gazeta,* November 10, 1962, p. 21.

[3] T. Khachaturov, *Voprosy ekonomiki,* 1963, No. 11, p. 31.

[4] Iu. Cherniak, *Planovoe khoziaistvo,* 1963, No. 8, p. 53.

There appear to be at least two excellent reasons for this anti-climactic action. First, despite or perhaps because of its mass of detail, the *Tekhpromfinplan* tends to be unrealistic and to lack consistency right from the start. Out of one thousand such documents recently examined by Soviet economists, not a single one was found to be balanced out and internally consistent. Another difficulty is that the planners are attempting, as it were, to use a snapshot, taken once a year, where a continuously working movie camera is needed. The economy, especially such a dynamic one as the Soviet, does not stand still. "Life alters plans every month, every week. Meanwhile, it takes no less than two or three months to recompute the *Tekhpromfinplan* of a typical machine-building factory with its 30 to 40 thousand indicators."[5]

The supply plan is another important lever of control in central planners' hands. As a general rule, Soviet enterprises are not allowed to sell producer goods to each other except by previous authorization and in amounts prescribed by higher authorities. Each summer the enterprise files with a regional *Sovnarkhoz* (Economic Council) a request (*zaiavka*) for the various supplies it will presumably need during the next year. Negotiations take place, in the course of which the original requests are usually pared down, consolidated and sent to republic ministries. In the case of some 18,000 commodities deemed to be of a national importance, final coordination and allocation take place at the central level, by Gosplan and the Sovnarkhoz U.S.S.R. The downward flow of commands takes place and eventually each enterprise is provided with buying permits and selling orders which enable it to conclude contracts with suppliers. This system was designed to prevent direct, uncoordinated dealings among the enterprises and is quite effective in that: "The buyer is separated from the seller by a long barrier of agencies and organizations. . . . For example, documents concerning distribution of tires pass through 32 echelons, ball bearings through 20 agencies. . . . Each time plans are changed, this long process is repeated."[6] The prohibitive amount of paperwork involved may be gathered from the well-publicized experience of the Moscow automobile plant named after Likhachev. The documentation required for it to obtain its annual supply of ball bearings from the adjacent GPZ factory weighs over 400 pounds and is handled by 14 agencies.

After this laborious process is completed, the Likhachev factory will obtain the permit to buy the ball bearings it needs. But will it

[5] *Ibid.* See also *Izvestia*, May 30, 1963, p. 3.

[6] N. Razumov, *Voprosy ekonomiki*, 1963, No. 7, p. 129.

now get the ball bearings? This is by no means certain. In fact, its supplier, the GPZ factory, received as many as 4,000 complaints about the non-delivery or delayed delivery of ball bearings during the first six months of 1963. Persistent shortages of ball bearings have been reported throughout the country, and in some cases led to work stoppages of entire factories. The fault was attributed to errors and miscalculations in the supply plans. The same is true of various other producer goods that are centrally allocated. In the Soviet economy, which is run without adequate inventories and reserves, any such shortage tends to spread — through what might be called a "bottleneck multiplier" — to higher stages of production, where it gives rise to magnified losses. For example, due to a miscalculation in the supply of fanbelts, tens of thousands of tractors and trucks remained idle last year and grain went unharvested. The cumulative loss to the economy may thus be out of all proportion to the value of the original item and "for lack of a nail" a production battle may be lost. According to Professor V. V. Novozhilov, malfunctioning of the supply system costs the Soviet industry each year roughly 25 per cent of its potential output. No wonder. How can a plant manager present detailed requests for next year's supplies and equipment before knowing what products his factory will be asked to turn out and in what amounts? Even if coordination of data at the subsequent stages of the bureaucratic process were perfect and if each supplier adhered strictly to his plan, shortages would still persist as long as the paper pyramids are erected on such shaky foundations.

III

Some generalization can now be made about the informational aspects of Soviet economic planning. The planners obviously attempt to obtain extremely detailed information from the enterprises and to direct their activities in equally minute detail. Professor Birman, Pro-rector of the Moscow Institute of National Economy, characterizes this approach as "the vicious attempt to gather in one document a whole ocean of commodities and to track the flows of each of them down from the center, . . . an attempt to anticipate and plan each motion a worker makes, each turn of the screw."[7]

The system's ability to handle and digest the required data appears to be taxed to the limit. Data are collected and processed by seventeenth-century methods, complains Academician Liusternik. "Central planning agencies get literally drowned in the avalanches of documentation." And an expensive drowning it is: over ten million

[7] *Ekonomicheskaia gazeta,* March 30, 1963, p. 7.

specialized officials are engaged in collecting and processing economic data.[8] At the same time that central planners are "drowning in an ocean of data," they nevertheless suffer from a shortage of information. The knowledge which they ultimately distill from that ocean is largely of the wrong kind; it is useless or inadequate for making those crucial choices which, in the Soviet economy, they alone can make. It enables them to determine the emplacement of each nail in a new steel mill. But should the steel mill have been built in the first place? "Knowledge is power," but only to the extent that it renders the decision-maker aware of the various alternative courses of action open to him and of their probable implications.

From this viewpoint, the ultimate yield of the "avalanches of data" descending upon the Soviet planners is less than modest. Thus, at best, only two or three alternative variants of the annual national economic plan are considered by the planners before their final choice is made. Academician Gnedenko points out that "one cannot even talk of selecting the optimum variant" under these conditions.[9] And its companion piece, the national supply plan, is prepared in only one or two variants.

In his important speech of February 14, 1964, Premier Khrushchev describes the way in which the key output and investment decisions were taken by Gosplan. "A circle, in geometry, is divided into 360 grades. Suppose now that these 360 parts are all apportioned among committees, ministries and departments of Gosplan, each of which takes care of only the segment allotted to it." Then, apparently, the agency in charge of "a segment" sets its output goal for the next year simply by mechanical extrapolation of its average rate of growth over recent years. Investment funds were apportioned among industries by similar means. Bureaucrats in charge of these crucial decisions often wear departmental blinkers and neglect interrelationships among sectors and products. Unbelievable as it may seem, even production of tires was planned without reference to the output of motor vehicles.

Setting targets by extrapolation obviously favors the established industries and products and impedes innovation. This conservative bias makes shifts in priorities, as set by the political leaders, difficult to implement. Khrushchev has related the difficulties encountered on that count in implementing the crash program of expansion of the

[8] N. Kovalev, *Voprosy ekonomiki,* 1962, No. 8, p. 101; G. Pirogov, *Planovoe khoziaistvo,* 1963, No. 8, p. 49.

[9] B. Gnedenko, "Pro matematichni metody v ekonomichnykh doslidzhenniakh," *Ekonomika radianskoi Ukrainy,* 1960, No. 4, p. 80. See also *Izvestia,* November 7, 1963, p. 3.

chemical industry launched in 1958.[10] The bureaucratic Franken-
stein created in order to impose the leaders' preferences upon the
economy has developed distinct preferences, momentum and inertia
of its own. Trotsky's predictions are coming true.

Khrushchev's vitriolic attacks on Gosplan's methods, the far-
reaching administrative reorganization of the economy following the
November 1962 Plenum, the virtual scrapping of the Seven Year
Plan in June 1963 and the enactment of the new Two Year Plan —
all have dramatized the extent of the malfunctioning of the economy
and the top leadership's recognition of the need for reform. What,
then, has been prescribed to cure the ailment?

An influential group of conservatives among the Soviet planning
executives and economists, while agreeing that the present system of
planning does not work satisfactorily, attribute its failure to insufficient detail of information received and orders issued by the planners.
They argue accordingly that the use of prices as the basis for decisions should be further restricted and replaced by ever more detailed
calculations in physical terms. Decisions concerning the assortment
and quality of the product which are still largely left to the managers
should be taken away from them. But who would handle the huge
volume of data required for this attempt to anticipate and program
everything in advance? The centralizers have a ready answer: high
speed electronic computers would do the job.

There is some truth in the centralizers' diagnosis but not in their
prescription. Academician Nemchinov points out that since Soviet
prices fail to reflect the actual cost of resources, managerial incentives based on them often work at cross-purposes and "those commodities which are in shortest supply are also often the least profitable for
the enterprises to produce." But, after all, the existing prices and
incentives are of the planners' own making and could be redesigned
so as to assure that, to quote Professor Liberman, "what is good for
the national economy would also become profitable for the enterprise."[11] Instead, the centralizers propose to eliminate the existing
feedbacks altogether and advocate an attempt to program in advance,
from the center, "each motion a worker makes, each turn of the
screw. . . ."

This attempt is utopian. As V. M. Glushkov has recently shown,
it implies that the central planners would have to consider several
quintillion relationships among the various products, probably the

[10] N. S. Khrushchev's speeches, *Izvestia,* November 20, 1962; April 24, 1963;
June 29, 1963.

[11] Liberman's proposals are discussed in M. I. Goldman, "Economic Controversy in the Soviet Union," *Foreign Affairs,* April 1963.

largest integer ever considered in economic analysis. Glushkov adds that even if high-speed electronic computers performing 30,000 operations a second were harnessed to that task, it would require one million computers working without interruption for several years.[12] And, of course, the economy would not remain frozen, waiting for the computations to be completed.

Glushkov's picturesque illustration dramatizes the fact that the Soviet economic bureaucracy cannot be catapulted from the seventeenth into the twentieth century by the mere use of electronic computers. Academician Berg compares it to the effort to modernize a spade by attaching an electric motor. "The organizations which computers are supposed to eliminate," writes another critic, "try instead themselves to apply the computers. . . . The existing system of economic information just cannot be adapted to new conditions."[13]

The well-known Liberman proposals are in fact extremely moderate compared to others which have thus far passed unnoticed in the West. Liberman's central idea is: let the enterprise decide how to produce, once the planners have told it *what* to produce. Under this scheme, the higher authorities would continue to set output and assortment goals for each enterprise, decide who buys what products and ration out material supplies. A prohibitive amount of paperwork would still be required. To paraphrase Birman, while the Central Planning Board would no longer have to track down "each motion a worker makes," it would still have to calculate the orbit of each nut and bolt manufactured in the Soviet Union and to regulate the quintillions of relationships resulting therefrom.

Birman's own proposals for reform are perhaps the most far-reaching of all. He proposes to do away with all physical output targets except for two or three dozen key products such as steel, oil, electric power. For all the other millions of products the enterprise itself would decide what to produce so as to maximize its profits on the basis of orders received from wholesale trade and from industrial consumers. Central allocation of producer goods would be abolished. Instead, enterprises would be permitted to purchase materials and machinery directly from producers at government-fixed prices. Enterprises would compete for orders rather than evade them. Automatic self-regulation by the forces of the buyers' market would replace the present system of guaranteed sales and uncertain supplies. The enterprises' compliance with the planners' broad goals would be assured

[12] V. M. Glushkov, "Ekonomika i kibernetika," *Vestnik akademii nauk* SSSR, 1963, No. 10, p. 11 f.

[13] G. Kh. Popov, "Elektronnaia sistema ekonomicheskoi informatsii," *Vestnik moskovskogo universiteta*, 1962, No. 5, p. 29, 21.

primarily by indirect regulation through prices, incentives, credit and financial policies, rather than by direct controls and communications with each manager.

An enormous saving would thus be achieved in terms of the information flows, of the amount of knowledge the planners would have to obtain and transmit. Except for the few products already mentioned, the central planners' task would be largely limited to setting the optimum proportions among the key aggregates — national income, investment, the rates of growth of the basic sectors and regions. In setting up these targets the planners would make wide use of mathematical models constructed with the aid of electronic computers.

IV

This step from muddling through to modeling would greatly improve the effectiveness of Soviet economic planning. Instead of the present two or three variants of the national economic plan, a great many alternative courses of action could be appraised. The plan finally selected would be far more likely to assure the fulfillment of the planners' preferences at the lowest possible cost. The planners would then be dealing with the proper subjects for decision and policy. Substantial decentralization of decision-making would be achieved but, in the final analysis, while sacrificing most of their rights to receive reports and issue orders, the planners might actually have more knowledge and correspondingly more power.

How would this power be used? The focus of the debate shifts increasingly to the fundamental questions: Who is going to make the decisions? Whose preferences are the plans to implement? Until recently, discussion of these topics would have been unthinkable. Mathematical economists were going out of their way to emphasize that they intended to use their models solely in order to suggest the most economical ways of reaching the planners' goals, without questioning or analyzing the goals themselves.

But, in the light of Khrushchev's remarks upon Gosplan's targeting methods, the planners' preferences turned out to differ from and even to conflict with those of the political leadership. The implications of this state of affairs were not lost upon the mathematical economists. At a recent conference a mathematician, V. A. Volkonskii, objected to the view expressed by a conservative economist, Boiarskii, that the model-builders should take decisions on ends as given and limit themselves to the search for optimum means of reaching these predetermined ends. This would mean, Volkonskii argues, "leaving such decisions to the practitioners, without any attempt at theoretical justification."[14]

But what is the proper theoretical basis for making decisions on ends? Why, for example, should one product-mix be chosen in preference to other possible combinations of products? Volkonskii proposes "the democratic approach" to this key decision. The planners should ascertain what are the actual preferences of the majority of the population and follow them — an implicit reinstatement of the principle of consumer sovereignty.

The very fact that these sensitive topics can now be publicly discussed by scholars throws revealing light upon the extent of relaxation of political controls in that area. In the past, political leaders had jealously guarded their monopoly with respect to decisions on ends against any infringement, real or imagined, on the part of economists. A whole generation of brilliant pioneers of mathematical economics perished during the first Five Year Plan, having been accused of "mathematical deviation in planning," of wanting "to crank out the plan's goals" with their desk calculators. In his letter to Yaroshenko, Stalin specifically excluded any problems of economic planning from the area in which economists were allowed to roam.

But times have changed. The present generation of mathematical programmers has more to offer than the early pioneers of the twenties. Computers have taken the place of desk-calculators, highly sophisticated econometric methods have been developed. And, if economists have more to offer, leaders have now less to lose since various key decisions on goals have, in the course of time, slipped anyway into the hands of the Gosplan bureaucrats. In this predicament, the leadership may be inclined to utilize the economists' expert knowledge and to let them participate in some of the basic decisions on ends. This is implied in Khrushchev's announcement, on February 14, 1964, of the creation of a new council to be composed of scientists and economists, along with political leaders and planning practitioners, which will deal with key decisions on economic and technical progress.

What are the probable effects of the various reforms in planning methods proposed by Soviet scholars? A Western observer tends naturally to sympathize with the would-be reformers' courageous efforts, in the expectation that they would promote efficiency, rationality and freedom of choice. How justified are such expectations?

Mathematical economists believe that the substitution of programming methods for rules of thumb in Soviet planning would raise the

---

[14] *Problemy optimal' nogo planirovania, proektirovania i upravlenia proizvodstvom,* Moscow, 1963, p. 502–504.

aggregate product by at least 50 percent.[15] Conjectural as such estimates are, the efficiency with which the Soviet system operates would
undoubtedly be greatly improved. We would be well advised, however, to keep in mind that rationally allocated resources may serve
highly irrational ends. Indeed, to the extent that we mistrust the
Soviet ends, it might be "rational" on our part to root for the all-out
centralizers ridiculed by Birman. Their attempts to plan everything
would soon turn everyone into a planner. And an economy à la
Glushkov where everyone is engaged in paperwork may not be
efficient but is, at least, likely to be peaceful.

The crucial decisions remain, therefore, those on ends, and here
the participation of Soviet scholars may have a humanizing influence.
It is significant that their first venture into this long forbidden area
resulted in Volkonskii's eloquent plea for respecting consumers'
choices.[16] It would be wrong to believe that all mathematical programmers are likely to share Volkonskii's concern for democratic
principles. Computers might well be used in order to invade the still
remaining areas of privacy and freedom. Thus, P. P. Maslov envi-
sions a mathematical model of the utilization of people's lives,
compiled in terms of man-days of life, work, rest and self-education,[17]
clearly an invaluable tool in the hands of a government that has
never been reluctant to utilize lives for its purposes. Absolute
knowledge may corrupt absolutely.

The ultimate effect which planning by computers may have on
the freedom of producers' choice is as conjectural as in the case of
consumer choice. Birman's vision of a partly decentralized economy
where important choices are left to the plant managers' initiative may
not be borne out by future events. The use of computers in American industry has, in many cases, promoted centralization. Whatever
these ultimate effects may be, the current transition from charismatics
to mathematics in Soviet economic planning is bound to have a
profound influence upon its efficiency, upon the style of leadership
and the economic climate of the country.

[15] *Trudy nauchnogo soveshchania po primenenii matematicheskikh metodov
v ekonomicheskikh issledovaniakh i planirovanii*, Vol. I, Moscow, 1961, p. 126.
It is interesting to note that Novozhilov attributes at least one-half of this potential gain to the improvement in informational efficiency of planning which the
use of mathematical methods would make possible.

[16] Another straw in the wind is the publication in *Pravda* (February 24 and
25, 1964) of an article by Professor A. Arzumanian, an economist, questioning
the prevailing policy of a preferential growth of heavy industry.

[17] *Voprosy filosofii*, 1962, No. 3.

PART FOUR

PROSPECTS FOR CONVERGENCE

INTRODUCTION

The distinguished Dutch economist Jan Tinbergen believes that the Communist and free economies are converging in several ways. "On the one hand each system is learning from experience and trying to overcome some of its own weaknesses. On the other hand, the systems begin to influence each other more and more." The realization, in command economies, of the need for specialized management, differential incomes as incentives, money values, interest as a cost element, free consumer choice, mathematical methods of planning and of international trade can all be considered to have changed these economies in the direction of free economies. In the latter, the size and roles of the public sector and of taxes have been expanded, free competition limited, education made more widely available, market forces eliminated or modified in some highly unstable markets such as agriculture, more planning introduced, and some form of price and wage controls as antiinflationary tools have been instituted.

While the differences between the two systems remain large, Professor Tinbergen believes these are diminishing.

Danish economist, Knud Erik Svendson takes issue with Tinbergen. Svendson argues that the decentralization reform under Khrushchev, by weakening the hold of powerful ministers in Moscow, increased the power of the Communist party at the local and territorial levels. But the Communist party, he claims, does not constitute an economic institution in Tinbergen's economic model even though it is not very helpful to discuss the Soviet economy without discussing the role of the Communist party in it.

116

The Soviet economy may be run more and more by managers, but the managerial roles are not the same as in a market economy. In Svendson's view collective ownership of the means of production and "the Soviet organization and planning model" continue to provide "greater possibilities for flexibility" for organizational and technological innovation "than an oligopolic structure based on private ownership" and "it is not correct to restrict these [attributes], as Tinbergen does, to a matter of the democratizing of higher education, the number of engineers, research grants on the budget, and so forth."

Even if the two systems were to converge in terms of the organization and operation of firms and price mechanism and even if consumer goods output were to increase to high levels comparable to Western market societies, the systems might continue to coexist rather precariously. That a rich Communist is more peaceful than a poor one is a tenuous proposition. Interestingly, this proposition seems to be popular among many who also believe that a fat capitalist is a bully and a weak capitalist (a small businessman) is safe or even good. However, wealth has not always produced peaceful people; nor has poverty always led to aggressiveness.

But even if wealth did produce placid and peaceful attitudes in market societies, its consequences in command societies would remain unpredictable. More wealth can mean more guns or more butter. And even if an increasing proportion of this wealth were to be devoted to consumer welfare, this is likely to be done more by increasing collective rather than private consumption.[1] Just as the consequences of collective ownership and production have been radically different from those of private ownership and production, the social, economic, cultural, and political results of collective affluence may turn out to be grossly different than those expected from private affluence.

It is particularly wishful to believe that as systems or societies become similar the friction between them will diminish. Jews and Arabs, Indians and Pakistanis, Catholics and Protestants, Trotskyites and Stalinists should by that token have been the best of friends.

---

[1] For one discussion along these lines see Jan S. Prybyla, "The Convergence of Western and Communist Economic Systems: A Critical Estimate," *The Russian Review*, Jan. 1964, pp. 3–17; also, Peter Wiles, "Will Capitalism and Communism Spontaneously Converge?" *Encounter* (London), June 1963, pp. 84–90.

JAN TINBERGEN

Do Communist and Free Economies Show a Converging Pattern?*

WE ARE witnessing today the coexistence of two radically different economic systems, the "communist" and the "free" economies (according to western terminology) or the "socialist" and "capitalist" systems (according to the eastern vocabulary). The various names given to them are far from precise. Perhaps the most imprecise thing about them is the suggestion that each of these systems represents something well-defined and hence invariant. Reality shows both to be in permanent change. Analysis of the nature of this change can prove quite fascinating. This essay proposes to show that the changes are in many respects converging movements. As will be seen, our essay is a very brief sketch only, trying to indicate a few main tendencies and not going into any detail, or, for that matter, into differences between the communist countries.

The main forces behind the changes may be brought under two broad headings. On the one hand each system is learning from experience and trying to overcome some of its own weaknesses. On the other hand the systems begin to influence each other more and more. While in the beginning the communist system was not taken seriously by the free system this has changed to a considerable extent. The communist system has been interested in some "capitalist" achievements from its very start. Now it is not so much imitating some of the western methods as learning economics from its own experience.

2. Some of the major changes which have occurred in the communist system since the Russian revolution will very briefly be summarized in this section:

(i) For a short while it was thought that specialized management was superfluous and that "the workers" could take care of this activity. It was soon learned that specialization is more efficient with regard to management. In fact, the traditional principle of resistance to specialization in all forms is becoming increasingly less prevalent.

* From Jan Tinbergen, "Do Communist and Free Economies Show a Converging Pattern?" *Soviet Studies*, Vol. XII, No. 4 (April 1961), pp. 333–341. Reprinted by permission of Basil Blackwell Publisher.

(ii) For a short while an attempt was made to equalize incomes in a drastic way. The well-known consequences of such equalization by decree forced the regime to introduce a wage system which makes wages largely dependent on productivity. Strangely enough, this was then labelled "socialist wage policy."

(iii) For some time planning was done in terms of physical quantities and not in terms of money values. Gradually the use of money as a common denominator penetrated into the planning system and the significance of prices and costs was more and more recognized.

(iv) For a long time interest was considered an unnecessary concept as a consequence of the elimination of private ownership of capital goods. Gradually it was discovered that the elimination of interest as a form of private income does not mean that it should also be disregarded as a cost element.

(v) Rationing was abolished a few years after the Second World War and free consumer choice accepted as a proper institution. Gradually some more emphasis was given to consumption as the purpose of production.

(vi) Mathematical methods of planning, considered as "capitalist" for a long period, were recently recognized to be objective and helpful and are now widely discussed and applied.

(vii) A profound change is under way in the concepts of international trade, not only between communist countries but also between communist and free economies. The idea that each country should have its own heavy industry is no longer adhered to.

3. The so-called free economies have also undergone thorough changes, which will now be summed up.

(i) The public sector nowadays is considerably larger than it was in the nineteenth century. Especially in western Europe public utilities are publicly owned; railways and tramways, coal mines, steel works, insurance companies and banks are often in the public sector.

(ii) The amount of taxes levied in western economies, often in the neighbourhood of one quarter of national income, means that taxes are among the important regulators of economic activity. In addition a considerable portion of the nation's savings is made in the public sector.

(iii) Free competition has been limited in many ways as a natural consequence of some technical forces (high fixed costs of production). It has also been voluntarily restricted by such movements as the drive for standardization.

(iv) Partly as a consequence of (iii) governments have limited the freedom of entrepreneurs by anti-trust laws.

(v) Access to education has been given gradually to an increasing portion of the population, often by providing education without charge. Moreover, education has been made compulsory up to a certain age.

(vi) Market forces have been eliminated or modified in some particularly unstable markets, especially in agriculture and in some cases even international commodity agreements have been concluded.

(vii) Planning has gradually been given an increasingly important role, both in big private enterprises and in the design of national economic policy.

(viii) Deliberate development policies have been in existence for a long time. In the nineteenth century already, transportation facilities were often created with public help. At present a whole range of measures, from tax facilities to government investments in infrastructure as well as in manufacturing industry proper, are applied to further the development of remote areas or poor regions.

(ix) Some forms of price and wage control as a direct means to prevent inflation have been used recently in a few "free" economies.

4. Several of the changes recorded above are in fact bringing the communist and the free economies closer together. This cannot be said, however, to mean that the differences are already small. There are very large differences still. But the process has not stopped. Both types of economies are facing many problems. They will have to move further. In this section we try to give a picture of the most striking differences still in existence and in the subsequent sections of the most important problems to be solved in both types of economies.

(i) The most striking difference is, of course, the size of the public sector. It should not be forgotten, however, that the power of the private sector in western countries is not commensurate with its formal size. In many indirect ways western societies have reduced this power. For example, taxes take away almost half of the profits. Of the remainder, a large part is invested and only a small part paid out as dividends. Western as well as communist economies are to a large extent dominated by managers. In the west, shareholders are no longer powerful. Social legislation in many respects also restricts the freedom of action of private entrepreneurs. So do a number of regulations with regard to quality control, pollution of water and air, building activity, town and country planning and so on.

(ii) Another important difference is the degree of freedom in production decisions. Factory managers in the west have much more freedom in this respect than managers in communist countries where a still very large number of items is planned centrally.

(iii) Accordingly, there is a considerable difference in the degree of detail in which the future course of the economy is planned in communist countries and in "free" economies. This refers to production as well as, e.g., to foreign trade.

(iv) Prices are controlled centrally in the communist countries to a much higher degree than in western countries, where, as a rule, only a few agricultural prices are under direct control. Here again, however, western countries use more indirect means of influencing prices. Among these, competition is the main institutional means, but import duties and monetary policies and (in Holland) wage control and price control of some other items are supplementary instruments.

(v) Industrial democracy is very different in the two types of countries. In the west only some beginnings have been made with co-determination of workers or their organizations in some social issues. In the communist world workers are given opportunities to participate in the discussions about the economic plans of the enterprise and about the use of a portion of the enterprise surplus.

(vi) Education constitutes another subject in which there is still considerable difference. In the "free" countries a certain portion of the potential students of secondary and university training cannot receive the education they need for lack of financial means. The portion is declining, however, as a consequence of several types of financial help, which in some countries enable as much as half of the student body to carry on their studies.

(vii) The differences in the level of savings are recently less striking between such countries as the continental European countries and the communist countries than they were before. Savings of about 20% of national income are now no exception in these western countries; Japan is saving nearly 30%. The United States and the United Kingdom, however, save considerably less.[1]

(viii) Regarding the principles of the international division of labour and the priorities of investment projects the differences between east and west are rapidly disappearing.

5. Corresponding to these problems the communist countries may have to face the following issues:

(i) A major problem seems to be the question of whether or not a gain in efficiency will result from making a large number of small

---

[1] One may comment that probably the U.S. and the U.K. are the most mature economies among the western countries. Interestingly enough, however, continental Europe used to have the same low savings rate as the U.K. and the U.S. for a long time, but after 1950 showed a remarkable increase.

enterprises in essence "private" enterprises by some sort of lease or concession system. If one tries to imagine the volume of administration now usual, say, in shops, it must be a burden on general efficiency.

(ii) A second major problem seems to be whether or not more freedom in production decisions can be given to managers. With rising real incomes citizens of the communist countries will require a finer pattern of qualities and assortment which it is hardly possible to plan centrally. Those closest to the market can probably best judge the needs. There does not seem to be any danger of the central authorities losing control over general economic development as a consequence of granting this type of freedom for the individual manager.

(iii) One also wonders whether or not the number of items planned centrally should be diminished in order to relieve the central planning agencies of a heavy burden which appears to have relatively unimportant qualifications in terms of increments in national well-being produced. The same may well apply to international trade planning.

(iv) The next question communist countries might put to themselves relates to price fixing. What harm is there in permitting prices to move as a consequence of relative shortages or abundances and letting them contribute to restore equilibrium? Is not such a method in fact quicker than a mere adaptation in production programmes or stocks? Prices will have to move anyhow as a consequence of technical progress and changes in crops. It remains an open question whether the changes should be permitted to individual sellers or only to central authorities. In other words, there seems to be a choice here where the answer is not so clear beforehand and where there is an element of discretion.

(v) A very fundamental question, going far beyond economic institutions is of course the one about a possible widening of democracy in our sense. It is not within the scope of this essay to make any speculations on this important subject.

6. Certainly the "free" economies also have to face questions.

(i) Has the public sector the correct size? In the United States important commentators have made the point that it is too small in that country and that recently some public tasks have been neglected.

Even if in European countries the question does not seem to be a controversial issue, the related question of how further to restrict the privileges of some forms of private income or capital still is one under discussion. There is an interesting argument about the possibility of restricting consumption financed out of capital gains, introduced by Nicholas Kaldor's book on "An Expenditure Tax." Possible restrictions on the income paid to directors are discussed and the case for higher inheritance taxes has not been decided upon. The impression of a certain stagnation in the reforms in this field is due not so much to general satisfaction about the present state of affairs as it is to the fact that progressive political parties are re-thinking their programmes.

(ii) There is not much debate in western countries about restricting the freedom of decisions of managers about their production programmes. Rather there is an increasing interest on the side of management for general economic forecasts and market analysis to help them in their decisions.

(iii) Accordingly the case for some more planning is a living issue in the west. One government after the other feels it has to do something in this field. The most recent example is Belgium, with a possibility for Germany to follow. In Asian countries planning is generally accepted; only the methods differ. The borderline European and Asian country, Turkey, has just established a planning agency. Latin American countries are one after the other engaging in some planning. There is a wide variation in the degree of detail planned and the time has come to discuss in a more precise way which degree of detail is the most appropriate. The outcome of such a discussion may also have its value for the communist countries.

(iv) Price formation is an issue of discussion in the west mainly when the general price level is at stake: should not governments have more instruments to counteract inflationary price rises, especially of the cost-push type? The existing situation is unsatisfactory. The use of only monetary and financial means contains the danger of creating unemployment before the price level goes down. Wage control as an indirect means of controlling prices is not accepted. International integration in order to strengthen competition may give some help in small countries, but does not solve the problem for larger countries. It may therefore be that after all some new form of price setting is necessary.

(v) There is a continued pressure in western countries to facilitate the access to education for larger groups of the population. Some of the proposals are going into the direction of the communist solution, namly to pay a wage to the student. Other proposals are more traditional.

(vi) Industrial democracy is an unsolved question too. The attempts so far made in Western Europe differ from country to country. None is very satisfactory.

7. The picture given shows that communist as well as "free" countries have to solve some problems and that there may be further tendencies to a converging movement. This is true particularly for the main question about the degree of decentralization in production decisions and planning. It is to some extent also true for the process of price formation. It is less clear with regard to the formal side of property, but a distinction between formal property and the real situation must be made. As already observed, both the income from property and the freedom of decision with regard to its use have been strongly reduced in the west and the process may continue.

It is interesting to add a more theoretical analysis to the factual description already attempted. What does economic science have to tell us about the probability of a further convergency of the organization patterns? It is evident that economic science can only tell us something about the subject in so far as economic forces will determine the movements. Clearly in the past other than economic forces have been at work. Nevertheless, would it be denied that economic considerations are important both to communists and, let us say, to Americans?

The chapter of economic science we may first consult is welfare economics. In principle, it tells us about the conditions which the optimum pattern of organization of society has to fulfil. Its contents have long been considered a defence of the free enterprise system, but wrongly so. It is true that welfare economics show that uniform prices (i.e. absence of price discrimination) are among the conditions for maximum welfare. But these can be established just as well by a system of government-controlled pricing as by competitive markets.

Another proposition of welfare economics is that prices should be equal to marginal costs. This statement implies that for the activities characterized by high fixed costs and technical surplus capacity private enterprise cannot be the system leading to maximum welfare, unless two-part pricing be applied for these activities.[2] Even in the case where all enterprises in these branches of activity would apply two-part pricing the question might arise whether or not a more efficient administration of this system could be obtained if these enterprises were combined. This combination, in turn, in order not to degenerate into a super-monopoly should be in public hands. Socialization may be the best solution therefore for all the activities concerned.

[2] J. Tinbergen, "The Theory of the Optimum Regime," Selected Papers (Amsterdam, 1959), p. 264.

Similar remarks are valid with regard to activities showing external effects. It can be shown, at the basis of welfare economics, that activities of this kind should be carried out by integrated units; integrated, that is, with the producers or consumers whose wellbeing is affected by the external effects. Socialization may again be a solution.

In concrete terms, the most important activities falling under these two categories are about the same as those already socialized in Western European countries, namely public utilities, rail and air transportation, highway construction and education. Possibly also steel and coal should be added and perhaps other types of transportation.

A further subject relevant to welfare economics is taxes. Two principles are important: first, that there must be some form of income redistribution and second, that income tax is not the optimal way of doing so. The redistribution taxes should approach as much as possible the lump-sum type, i.e. the type not taxing marginal income. Wealth taxes are perhaps the nearest example we know today.

All this points to the desirability of some sort of a mixed system, as far as property is concerned, and to a tax system which may hit personal wealth more than it now does in the west. It also points in the direction of admitting more decentralization with regard to the activities showing constant or increasing costs, i.e. generally for industries where small units are justified as the communist countries may discover in the future.

8. Reference to another chapter (or chapters) of economics may be needed, in order to answer the following questions. What element of truth is there in the contention sometimes made that there is no optimum in the middle, but rather a tendency for optima to be at the extremes?

This opinion is sometimes illustrated by the argument that "once you start to deviate from market price formation you have to regulate more and more until the whole economy is regulated." Is this illustration relevant to our subject and would it, in a general way, disprove the assumption of an optimum somewhere halfway? The alleged tendency to divergency rather than convergency can no doubt be observed in some cases of war economy regulations. If you start rationing and price control in some markets you will soon find it necessary to regulate other markets too. The argument does not necessarily apply to other types of intervention, however. An interesting example to the contrary can be found in business cycle policy. Here it is generally accepted that if you regulate the total flow of demand by appropriate instruments — e.g. financial and monetary policy —

you may then leave most markets to themselves. You can, in addition, select a few markets showing characteristics of instability, which may be controlled without the necessity for controlling other markets. Those to be controlled are the ones showing long production lags or a long life of the products.

In the same manner the ownership of the means of production is not characterized as such by a tendency to spread. In Western Europe there exists a public sector of a certain size which has maintained itself for years without making it necessary to expand it rapidly in order to preserve some equilibrium. If in the U.S.S.R. private business has virtually vanished it is because it was discriminated against on ideological grounds and, in the initial period, for reasons of political power.

In the case of planning a similar position can be maintained. Planning the main elements of the economy does not necessarily imply the need for detailed planning.

It cannot be argued therefore that there is an inherent tendency for economic regimes to move to the extremes. Our theoretical reconnaissance therefore, seems to support rather than to undermine the views derived from observation. No doubt the optimum organization of the economy will differ from country to country and from period to period. It is also hardly conceivable that we will soon be able to indicate precisely where the optimum lies, or even to say whether "east and west" will actually "meet" in their attempts to find the "welfare summit."

9. This essay may be concluded with a few remarks about the "non-committed" countries, that is non-committed to one of the two economic systems at the extremes. Being underdeveloped countries at the same time, they still have a significant number of feudal elements. They are less subject to preconceived ideas about the economic system. If the state sector plays an important role in some of them it is because the necessary initiative was first taken in this rather than in the private sector (Turkey, India).

This group of countries is now facing some very urgent economic needs, partly as a consequence of increasing contacts with the outside world, partly because they have only recently become independent states. The most pressing need is the one for a higher level of production. Another need is to live under a system of stabler prices. Several secondary aims of policy can be derived from these primary ones, such as the full use of resources, an increase in investment levels and a diversification of their production pattern.

Because of the presence, in today's world, of the two major

systems the underdeveloped countries are looking to both in order to learn from them. They are above all interested in rapid growth and less in such issues as parliamentary democracy, since they have hardly ever had it. The communist example impresses them greatly. Planning is in high esteem. State initiative does take up part of the tasks neglected by private initiative. The willingness to interfere with price formation is understandable since they are often depending on typically unstable markets. Conditions seem favourable in these countries to try to combine the best elements from communism and free enterprise. These countries therefore may become the experimental ground for economic regimes.

They may, as they sometimes do in technical matters, skip one phase in their development and at once aim at the best solution. They should try to. And we may follow with particular interest the pattern of society that is emerging.

KNUD ERIK SVENDSEN

Are the Two Systems Converging?*

THE TWO main types of economic systems, that of capitalism or private ownership and that of socialism or collective ownership, have in the course of time been submitted to such great changes that it is natural to ask in which direction they are moving.

Professor Jan Tinbergen's answer to this question is that the two systems are, in reality, undergoing a process which is bringing them closer together as institutional models. This opinion is also expressed in his earlier formulation of the need for a general economic theory common to all systems. Tinbergen has pointed out that the two system are not diametrical opposites but contain a series of common elements, that the transition from one system to the other takes place

* From Knud Erik Svendsen, "Are the Two Systems Converging?" *Øst-Økonomi* (December 1962), pp. 195–209, footnotes omitted. Reprinted by permission of *Economics of Planning*. Based on a part of an address at the 11th Scandinavian congress for younger national economists in Copenhagen, June 1962. Translated from Danish by *Jane Hamre*, Oslo.

gradually rather than by leaps and bounds. He has emphasized this in order to demonstrate that economists from both systems have common problems to discuss, and he considers it in the interest of peaceful co-existence to concentrate more on the similarities than on the differences and to avoid black-white conceptions.

Professor Tinbergen's motives are thus above reproach. Nor can there be any doubt that many of the changes which have taken place in East and West have contributed to bringing a part of the economic processes in the two systems closer to each other. My use of his article in *Soviet Studies* (April, 1961) as a basis for the following comments is therefore not intended to raise an open polemic against Tinbergen's viewpoint, but primarily to set forth the view that it is essential to stress the differences — among other things because it is through the dissimilarities that economists of the two systems presumably can best enlighten each other. In the second place, some of Tinbergen's arguments with regard to changes in the Soviet system are, in my opinion, not completely precise, and, in any case, bear examining. Finally, Tinbergen takes no notice of a series of economic phenomena which, it seems to me, are important in any consideration of the systems. Disagreement on this third point may possibly be traced to different limitations of the concept "economic system."

In his article in *Soviet Studies*, Tinbergen mentions the following as the most important changes in the communist system: (a) Recognition of specialists in administration, as opposed to the earlier policy, under which the workers were collectively responsible for leadership. (b) Introduction of wages based on productivity, not equal incomes. (c) More planning with monetary methods and greater recognition of the significance of prices and costs. (d) Greater understanding of the importance of interest as a cost. (e) Free choice for the consumer instead of rationing and, in recent years, more emphasis on consumption. (f) Increased understanding of the international division of labour.

After having analyzed the changes in the Western system, a problem which will not be treated in this article, Tinbergen maintains that there still are important differences between the systems and mentions as examples: (a) The importance of the official sector; despite this dissimilarity, both systems are, however, to a large extent controlled by managers. (b) Administrators in the West enjoy greater freedom in decisions concerning production. (c) Considerable difference in the extent of the details of planning. (d) Prices are more centrally controlled in the East, while Western countries rely more upon indirect methods to influence prices. (e) In the West there is only the embryo of an industrial democracy, while in the East the workers may participate in the discussion of practical plans. (f) In the West there is still limited opportunity for education.

It will be noted that one of the greatest changes in the Soviet economy within recent years, the so-called decentralization of industry, construction, etc., in 1957, is not directly taken into account in the above-mentioned changes. On the whole, there exists some uncertainty in the evaluation of this radical reform, where the individual firm's vertical grouping under industrial or branch management was replaced by a horizontal or territorial division under the approximately 100 economic councils (sovnarchozy). Can this properly be called a decentralization?

This uncertainty has its roots in the fact that in our "Western" interpretation of the concept "decentralization," it is the market as an economic organization model that dominates our minds. It is the market that binds together the individual economic units, household and business, supplies them with information, and coordinates their actions. And in relation to the enterprises, the industrial reform did not entail change in principle. The reform had no connection with the theoretical discussion concerning a socialistic model of competition, where only certain rules of procedure are imposed upon enterprises.

The reform was of course based upon economic arguments, namely that the breaking down of the partially self-supplying industrial imperiums and the formation of geographical units would reduce transportation expenses and lead to a better division of labour, and that the planners and administrators in the economic councils would have better knowledge of the enterprises than the ministries in Moscow. The position of the enterprises in relation to the economic councils would therefore differ from that to the ministry — in other words, a kind of decentralization, although not one consistent with the prevalent market concept.

That is to say, it is necessary to work with other patterns or organization than the market model, and this attempt has been made by several economists within past years. Here research workers in eastern affairs, like Robert W. Campbell, can point out that the Soviet economy with its many organizational mutations may serve as a laboratory for such exercises in organizational theory.

Let us, for example, consider the economic councils and their role in the system. Whose interest do they protect, and what is the norm for their behavior? They are, in the organizational scheme placed between the individual enterprises and the great planning commission in Moscow, whose authority was greatly expanded by the reform. It is the function of the councils to set forth for Moscow the regional interests without falling prey to special local interests and at the same time to press for better production results, so that they are not only passive representatives for the interests of the enterprises. They have a double role in the organizational scheme, just as the branch associations in the Polish model. There are many organizational arguments for such a situation, the consequences of which may not be described in ordinary market terminology.

There are naturally also political arguments. It was unquestionably intended that the reform should strengthen the influence of the local party organs (and therefore of Khrushchev). The party is territorially organized and local leadership often drew the shortest straw in competition with the powerful ministers in Moscow. The party's influence has thus been increased. But does the communist party properly belong in our economic model? Tinbergen, in any case, does not seem to accept it as an economic institution.

In reality, of course, the party apparatus plays an important part, not only in a political sense, but also in relation to economics. With respect to the individual enterprise, the office of the communist party has its role in the organizational scheme, just as the director and the trade unions have theirs. In the theoretical scheme, the party represents society's interests as opposed to the pure self-interest of the enterprise which it is the function of the director to attend to. It is therefore an important task to prevent any coalition between these different factions, and this may be done (among other methods) by frequent shifting of directors and party secretaries.

It may be contended that such considerations are not a part of economics, but without weighing problems of this type it is impossible to throw sufficient light on economic systems, whether these are dominated by large private enterprises or based on state control.

In order to understand the Soviet economic system, this consideration is especially significant. It has been and will probably continue to be a specific result of society's ownership of the means of production — combined with the Soviet political system — that it has been possible to carry out the various sweeping organizational changes, just as it has been an effect of the communist party's power that it was possible in 1958 with one blow to abolish the machine-and-tractor stations and sell the material to the collective farms, not to mention the radical unification of collective farms which since the war has halved their number.

It is clear that various group interests must get into conflict concerning such changes. Such specialized interests are not extinguished by collective ownership; but by a greater mobility, broader recruiting in the circles of leadership, and by organizational structures crossing each other the Soviet system provides greater possibilities for flexibility than an oligopolic structure based on private ownership.

Not everyone will agree with this evaluation. What is significant in Tinbergen's model description, however, is that one should not avoid treating problems of this kind.

One of Tinbergen's points, that both systems are to a large extent controlled by managers, is in any case an abstract oversimplification which does not appear to be sufficiently substantiated by the changes in the Soviet economy, not to mention that the term "manager" is far from satisfactorily defined.

The next question I shall consider is that of the character of planning. This is, as pointed out by Tinbergen, still centralized in the U.S.S.R. in the sense that the work of the central planning organs consists of more than harmonizing plans submitted by individual enterprises or economic councils. Actually our terminology on this point is also somewhat unclear. The central organs as well as the individual enterprises have influence in determining the goals. Empirically one may attempt to evaluate how much is dictated from above, more speculatively — by an analysis of the individual enterprises' power position — one may try to appraise the result of the negotiations. In the latter case, it is significant that the central organs have access to extensive information as to the internal circumstances within the individual enterprises. In this sense, from the point of view of the enterprises, the position of the economic councils is stronger than that of the ministries. Thus we have returned to organizational theory.

The same is applicable in a discussion of what the individual enterprise and its director shall maximize. We like to imagine that this is one simple, measurable quantity, for example, profit. The solution for the individual Soviet manager is not so obvious. Certainly it is first and foremost gross production, that is to say the value of production that is his "success indicator" — to use Alec Nove's expression — but at the same time he must satisfy a number of other targets in various plans, and he can never be certain as to what his superiors will find important in a given situation. Alec Nove has stressed that from an organizational standpoint this can be a useful principle. It increases the directors' ability to adjust themselves and hinders their being bound up bureaucratically in inflexible behavior patterns.

These remarks are just as important as the more normal comments on planning which we also find in Tinbergen's article: whether it occurs in physical units or in money, whether it is more or less detailed.

Soviet planning is primarily a matter of specifying production goals for the individual enterprises. The plans can be more or less specified in the assortment of goods, but they are concerned with the achievement of a certain production measured by fixed, or at any rate, by centrally determined prices. The enterprises' manoeuverability depends upon its freedom in the composition of production, and this is so slight that it would seem most accurate, as Tinbergen does, to call the planning physical, even though this terminology is also inadequate. Its freedom also depends upon its possibility of choice in methods of production. These too are limited; there is no free consumers' choice for means of production. The so-called material-technical supply distributes the inputs according to specific norms.

This discussion of the physical character of planning or of its details need, however, have no relation to the truly pertinent fact: that through the stipulation of goals pressure is brought upon the enterprises. It is inherent in the planning that the result shall improve from year to year.

This pursuit of increased gross production is called in the Soviet Union "the gross cult," and by making use of the negative results of this planning method, we in the western world have occupied ourselves particularly with its weaknesses.

Yet whatever its weaknesses, it remains that the plan exerts pressure. As enterprises in western countries attempt tax evasion, Soviet enterprises attempt "plan evasion" by concealing reserves etc. Still the taxes come in, and still production is pressed us. And this pressure lies in the direct planning, based on collective ownership, by which the directors of enterprises can be moved up or down in the state-owned industry's hierarchy.

Another characteristic of Soviet planning is that it builds upon cost comparisons among enterprises, what may be called production costs' transparency. This more or less perfect mastery of cost information naturally affects the planning process in a different manner than if the planning were undertaken with the maintenance of business secrets common in private enterprise.

The American economist David Granick, who has studied in particular the individual enterprise's position in the Soviet Union, has set forth the opinion that this position is of special interest where the Soviets can build on Western technique and apply it as quickly as possible to enterprises with inexperienced leadership. In his view it is quite another thing where it is a question of independent technique. It is doubtful whether he is correct in this assumption. The studies which American engineers have undertaken of the Soviet steel industry indicate precisely the great speed with which new technical improvements are spread within this state-owned industry. Although the steel industry is not typical for Soviet industry today, it is more indicative than the many examples of restrictive bureaucracy in other technical fields in the present Soviet Union, which may be explained by the generally lower stage of productivity.

It must, in any case, be assumed that the particular Soviet organization and planning model has special attributes in the question of technical progress. And it is not correct to restrict these, as Tinbergen does, to a matter of the democratizing of higher education, the number of engineers, research grants on the budget, and so forth. On the basis of collective ownership there may obviously be several different institutional arrangements with various capacities for spreading new techniques, but also in this field there is possibility for changing the organizational pattern radically, which has occurred in the past few years.

Let me conclude these comments on planning with some remarks on material incentives. It is unnecessary to go into that comprehensive and constantly running discussion as to the device of bonus systems etc. The principle is that these incentives should be applied in a manner that will support the planned goals. It is, of course, a problem that their existence can encourage the efforts to set up "easy" plans, but this may be counteracted by special bonus rules, if need be determined through experiments with various systems in different state enterprises.

These incentives have concerned Eastern research a great deal, and rightfully so. For we find in these incentives an extension of the market model, where the parameters are price and cost. Now it must be recognized that besides price rules there must also be created rules for incentives which, together with the price policy, may inspire the desired reaction from the enterprises. One of the problems brought up in the most recent discussion of incentives in the Eastern countries was exactly such a co-ordination of price and incentive systems that the desired result might be obtained regardless of whether or not the situation is decentralized as concerns the market.

As for prices, Tinbergen's comments on their rising importance and their centralized regulation are unquestionably correct. It is well known that in the past years the price problem has been hotly discussed, and that a thorough reform for industrial products (wholesale prices) is on the threshold. And it may be expected that better prices will not only affect the central planners in their choice of production methods and hence their allotment of inputs to the individual enterprises, but also that the individual enterprises will enjoy more freedom as concerns substitution of production factors. It has, at least, been set forth recently by a leading economist in Gosplan's department for this distribution system that an abandonment of the licenses will be attempted in the course of $2-3-4$ years. Within that time the system will have been improved by the building up of stocks, and will leave the sellers' market which has plagued the suppliers of individual enterprises for many years.

A moderation of this kind will mean a reduction of the details in planning and will increase the freedom of enterprises to the most radical extent in the history of Soviet planning. Somebody will perhaps claim that it will change the model completely. However this is interpreted, such a freedom of substitution or consumers' choice for the enterprises will not alter the plan's character of growth pressure. The enterprises will continue to be pressed for better results, but assurance of the proper choice of goods or output-mix will be transferred to the market with its threat of difficulties in selling, an unknown phenomenon for Soviet enterprises to date.

For the sake of accuracy it should be stated that the preliminary work on price reforms is not co-ordinated with the Western price discussions, and for that matter is only slightly connected with the Eastern debate. Price regulators as a group apparently entertain little interest for price theory.

In relation to our theme it is, however, more interesting to raise the question as to how prices can be used in the more farsighted planning. It is a commonly held opinion that to obtain a maximum of welfare, prices should be fixed in proportion to marginal costs. If changes occur in the demand, prices should be regulated accordingly; if the marginal costs change, prices should be modified too, so that the proper proportion is maintained. In this model, the main function of the planning organs will be to fix these equalizing prices.

This reasoning assumes that changes in demand or technique are exogenous. But is it possible to hold this viewpoint in connection with the planning organs?

It is in conflict with our values to imagine that the planners influence the demand. We should like the consumer to choose freely, that is without manipulation, and I shall therefore let this side of the case go undiscussed, even though it is clear that the political authorities in practice must remember that their acts actually do influence demand, whether or not this is the intention. An analysis of these questions can only lead to complex philosophical debates.

Let us rather, therefore, consider the costs. My standpoint here is that it is difficult to speak of endogenous technical changes in connection with research planning. Let me attempt to clarify the problem by an example: We assume, for the argument, that there exist only two consumer goods: clothing and food and that their prices at the outset are regulated according to maximum welfare. Now the organizers have to decide whether in their research program it is clothing or food which should be cheaper. We can thus theoretically conceive a series of sets of different marginal costs respectively for clothing and food and for each set a corresponding set of maximum welfare prices. Without directly influencing the demand, we have thus different situations of maximum welfare. Our basic rule concerning prices and marginal costs cannot help us here.

In other words, the marginal cost price rule is an inadequate welfare criterion, and one ought to look for other welfare disciplines. With this, I shall simply point out that the existence of "sensible" prices in a system is not so interesting as choice of the pattern of development, and that the Russian considerations of a "rational" consumption may not simply be thrust aside as paternalistic.

Tinbergen's remarks concerning the Soviet wage system overlook something of particular interest. The problem of equal wages as opposed to wages according to results stems from the early 1930's and has been decided, as Tinbergen mentions, in favour of productivity, however — and in this we diverge from Tinbergen — not only with repect to short-time productivity, i.e. remuneration per piece or according to progressive rates. To a high degree, the wage differences have had as their goal to be incentives to a higher education. The big differences in salaries are to a large extent based upon education — a new qualification guarantees a higher salary — and must therefore be appraised in relation to the manifold educational possibilities offered to the workers.

What is interesting in the Soviet wage system is therefore not that it is a piece rate system consistent with the socialist principle "to each according to his production," but that it is a part of a long-reaching educational policy. With the increase of the extent of basic education of the workers, the gap between the highest and the lowest wage groups has therefore also been narrowed.

In concluding this subject I may mention the remarks set forth by A. Aganbegian on the reduced working hours. Since the workers in 1960 have gone over to a 36 or 41 hour week, with an average week of 40,2 hours, it is planned to initiate a 30–35 hour week from 1964–1968. This occurs in a situation where the Soviet Union calculates that its productivity is no more than 40–50% of the American. And in the Western commentaries which look positively on this development it is considered as evidence of a high appraisal of leisure in comparison to productive work.

Aganbegian, however, puts forth a theory — supported by hypothetical figures with regard to the output in the final working hours — that this shortening of the working day will tend to raise the cultural-technical level of the worker. Working with machines requires, in his opinion, 7 years general school plus 1–2 years special education. Automation, on the other hand, demands 10 years general school and 3 years special education. It is therefore important that people should have time for this extra education. The efforts to open restaurants follow the same line: investigations in certain cities show that the female workers devote approximately 2 hours daily to the purchase and preparation of food, in other words to this end nearly 10 million yearly workers are used. Such a course of reasoning must surely have its effect on the price policy of the restaurants, which it undoubtedly has — and this may be cited as far-reaching consideration of external economies.

Another point concerning the wage scale is that wage differences are affected by the planning of the labour force. If the authorities decide that wages in the building branch — to take a chance example — are too high, they may seek to increase the number of workers in this trade, which can be accomplished in many ways, and not necessarily by use of force or regulation of wages. It presupposes to a certain extent that the trade unions are without influence in this respect, and that is somewhat characteristic of the Soviet situation.

If this is true, one might fix wages according to the above-named educational considerations. If one must take into account organizations, or if one wishes wages to have a different dimension as incomes than as costs for the enterprises, then it is possible, as suggested by L. V. Kantorovich to work with a double set of wages.

The one set is the basis for income payments, while the other figures in the cost calculations of the enterprise. Certain phenomena in the Soviet reality would force one to think in these terms without knowledge of Kantorovich's theoretical arguments. In addition to their cash wage, the workers obtain certain advantages more or less gratis. It was further proclaimed with the Third Communist Party Program in 1961 that this free distribution should be extended during the coming years as the beginning of the effecting of the communist principle: from each according to his ability, to each according to his need.

How these free meals and the low rents are to be financed is not known. It may be that they shall be debited the enterprises' books, as the housing projects have been to date. In the calculation of marginal costs, however, it is significant how this portion of the workers' actual income is to be financed. If necessary, a greater or lesser part must be looked upon as fixed costs, and this again will influence the combination of production factors.

This leads me to the discussion of the far-sighted perspective or, as it is termed in official language, the "creation of the communist society's material-technical basis."

Tinbergen does not touch upon these ideological questions. On the other hand, numerous researchers of recent years, among them the West German professor Karl G. Thalheim have raised the problem as to whether the economic question is about to become non-ideological in the Soviet Union, whether the system and its economic activities have become less bound by ideology. It is Thalheim's opinion that the proclamation of the transition to communism at the 21st Congress was a mark of stronger ideology in the Soviet economic system. In this instance, where a fundamental dogma comes into conflict with the economic "ratio," common sense is bound to lose.

Professor Thalheim's theory, however, builds upon a very narrow definition of the concept "Ideologiegebundenheit," namely the existence of two fundamental axioms: in the first place, the general rejection of all private ownership of the means of production, and in the second place, the conviction of the absolute superiority of central planning over market economy.

The development in the Soviet Union has demonstrated that on the basis of these two axioms a great variation of institutional character can exist. Last year's discussion on the future position of collective farms indicates clearly that also in the discussion of property rights there is considerable difference of opinion.

The basis for professor Thalheim's point of view is possibly the conviction that the capitalist system with its private ownership of the means of production is the only sensible one. From this standpoint, the Soviet system is certainly bound, that is to say burdened by its ideology.

It is also possible to consider "ideology" in a broader and more positive manner as an expression of social aims. The problem for Eastern researchers is then how much these planned goals which are expressed in the concept "the communist society" influence the social development, or whether this development is exclusively dictated by the material-technical stage of society.

Seen from this angle it is correct to state that the Soviet system is more ideological than previously in the sense that perspectives for the individual's existence rather than mere industrial growth have been accentuated in the new party program. It is wisest, in my opinion, to assume that the Soviet system — or, if you wish, its active core — is extremely target-minded.

It lies in the very nature of the collective ownership that such aims or social preferences are set up, and these preferences must, under the system, be looked upon as having the same value as individual preferences, as these are expressed on the consumer market. Not only is it clear that a great deal of economic activity takes place outside the market — this is true also of other systems — but the market is evidently affected by the economic policy and aims.

It may perhaps be expressed in this manner that the Soviet system is biased in favour of these social preferences, whereas what we may call the liberal society is biased in favour of private preferences. From the point of view of development strategy, the first is possibly superior.

This does not mean that any particular theory has been advanced in the Soviet Union for the setting up of these social preferences. In practice you find a centralized decision process without any theory as to how the central authorities reach their decisions.

The political effects of the change which the Soviet Union is undergoing must be sought in this field: how are these preferences fixed? Presumably there will occur certain changes in favour of market preferences, but it will undoubtedly continue to be a special attribute of the Soviet system that it in a large area will be based on social preferences.

My knowledge of the making of plans, of the industrial democracy as regards the single enterprise etc. in the Soviet Union is too limited to permit further discussion. However, as far as Poland is concerned, it is here that one meets the most interesting phenomena. The extensive Polish publicity on economic problems is not only dependent on the frankness of the ministries, and enterprises, but also on a staff of trained economic journalists and special councils where the leaders of enterprises, politicians, professional economists, journalists, and others can debate. This public debate is a necessary condition for a rational and democratic formation of targets. A complete comparison of the Eastern and Western systems would require that this macro-economic transparency of the two systems be brought under discussion.

CONCLUSION

The desire for rapid economic growth is becoming universal. Rising standards of living for people, increased military power and international prestige for nations and larger resources to influence the course of international events all depend on economic growth.

Systems in which the volume and composition of output and its distribution are determined largely by market demand are relatively new in human experience and represent a break with tradition.[1] They have transformed Western Europe's feudal and static societies into dynamic modern nations with high and rising standards of living. In the United States the market system, unhampered by a feudal heritage, rigid social stratification, and state-supported cartels, has produced the world's most affluent nation, which is still growing rapidly.

Traditional systems, often based on the command principle, serve to perpetuate the *status quo* rather than promote change. The most important command systems for promoting economic growth are the centrally planned economies in Communist states. The Soviet Union was the first nation to adopt such a system with the inauguration of the first Five Year Plan in 1928. These systems solve their economic problems by specifying in physical terms the volume and composition of output to be produced by firms, the mode of production in each firm, and the uses and distribution of this output. It is these we currently refer to as command systems, even though other command systems such as Nazism have existed in the recent past.

Command economies have generated very rapid economic growth. The first and paramount command economy, that of the U.S.S.R., grew for almost thirty years at a rate about twice as great as that of the leading demand system.[2]

During the two world wars the Soviet economy suffered heavy losses of capital manpower and other resources. Its output fell drastically. In the same two periods the American economy poured out goods at unprecedented rates to wage the wars, help the Allies, and

---

[1] Markets have always been present in history but an entire economy organized around the market principle is a revolutionary concept which came to full bloom first in England during the Industrial Revolution in the eighteenth century; see Robert L. Heilbroner, *The Making of Economic Society* (Englewood Cliffs, N.J.: Prentice-Hall, Inc., 1962), pp. 1–100.

[2] Gregory Grossman, "30 Years of Soviet Industrialization," *Dissent*, Spring 1959, pp. 150–160.

sustain civilian consumption at even higher levels. During peacetime, the Soviet rate of growth accelerated while the American rate slackened. Marxists see in this a confirmation of their belief that capitalism *needs* war and war expenditures as stimulants while socialism needs peace and disarmament. What this record does show, however, is that the major problem of demand systems has been the instability and insufficiency of the *volume* of demand, though they are very efficient in producing goods to match the *pattern* of demand. Conversely, the command systems, by operating with full or over-full employment and by forcing high rates of saving and investment, have been able to offset the inefficiencies of command in peacetime. Faced with shortages in the volume of resources, the wasteful economic organization of the productive apparatus performs poorly. Even full employment, which should normally be considered an important indicator of macroeconomic efficiency, turns out to be a mixed blessing in such systems. The system of physical planning tends to encourage "hoarding" of labor, capital, raw materials, and other inputs by firms. A more efficient system of management, planning, and resource allocation would turn much of this "disguised unemployment" into open unemployment. In a rapidly changing economy, especially one which still has a very large population in the agricultural sector, there is bound to be some frictional, seasonal, and technological unemployment. These systems, however, refuse even to acknowledge the existence, much less to measure the extent, of such phenomena. Lack of information can only hurt efficient planning.

Not all Communist economies have produced faster growth than market economies. Japan, West Germany, and Israel have been the three leading economies for over a decade in terms of growth rates. Other market economies such as Sweden, South Africa, Mexico, and postwar Italy have grown for fairly long periods at rates comparable to those of the Communist systems. Nevertheless, the empirical comparisons of the Russian and American economies have strengthened a widespread belief that the Marxian ideology and/or authoritarian institutions are more productive of economic growth than the ideologies and institutions of free markets. Careful and systematic comparisons of a large number of countries, using uniform concepts of national output, are more likely to support Amlan Datta's judgment that "neither protestantism nor dialectical materialism nor any other special doctrine is essential to industrialization," nor are "any particular set of institutions necessary to economic growth."

In recent years, affluent demand systems have been evolving policies, institutions, and popular beliefs conducive to economic stabilization and growth; average annual growth rates in many have accelerated from the historic 2 to 3% to upwards of 5%, suggesting that economic maturity does not necessarily lead to decelerated growth. Indeed, the opposite has happened in the U.S., U.K., West Germany, Canada, France, and Japan. This is all the more remarkable since the United States has been trying to reduce agricultural output in the face of ever-increasing farm surpluses. Canada and France are also worrying about outlets for their mounting farm produce.

In spite of low levels of agricultural output and consumption in the command economies, growth of total output and productivity has been very disappointing, a good reason why protagonists of such systems should and often do focus on comparative rates of growth of *industrial* output. But in recent years even their industrial growth has been slowing down. During the last few years the Russian rate of growth seems to have declined from about 7% to about 2.5%, or only half of the American rate. This has lent support to those who want to reform the Soviet system.

The nature and intensity of recent discussion of economics in the command economies and experiments with new organizational patterns suggest that certain ideological barriers to the introduction of market prices, interest, profits, decentralized decision-making, consumers' "sovereignty," may wither away, paving the way for renewed vigor in the economies. As a result of some of these developments, the two systems have more operational similarities. If this trend continues, the two systems may cease to have significantly different rates of growth.

Again the experience of the recent past suggests that command systems have been, on the whole, slow in responding to the challenge thrown up by their decelerating growth. The speed with which institutional and policy innovations have been introduced in West Germany, the U. S., France, the Netherlands, Japan, the U. K., Austria, Sweden, Norway, and several other market economies suggests that the demand mechanism produces quick responses when a large number of people demand change. Command may be a more efficient mechanism for change when those to be commanded are politically and economically weak and the commanders have the political and economic power to enforce their command. But change is likely to be slower when it necessitates changing commanders, or their beliefs, privileges, and powers.

This view of the relation of command and change is consistent with the notion that command is an efficient instrument for achieving a limited number of goals such as growth in a poor and simple economy in which the elite know better than the ignorant masses, but it becomes increasingly inefficient as these conditions disappear. This view is gaining support even within the Soviet bloc countries. It should be easy to invoke doctrinal sanctions for the view: institutions and ideas that were progressive in one stage of economic growth become road blocks to be swept away to permit man's entry into a still better phase of history.

The engineers, the computer experts, the economists, the professional managers, and the professors—children of revolutionary planning—having grown up, want to retire their old, beloved and weakening parent who insists on running the household with her erstwhile iron grip.

Appealing and comforting as this view may be, the question remains whether or not centralized physical planning with all its attendant features of force, deprivation and cruelty is really necessary or even more efficient than a market system, for a poor economy wanting to grow rapidly.[3] The experience of Japan, Mexico, Israel, West Germany, and even communist Yugoslavia suggests the answer is "no." However, nations, like men, like to learn from their own experience rather than of others. In any event, the choices between command and demand mechanisms are seldom made for reasons of economic growth alone.

---

[3] For a somewhat similar theme see Alec Nove, *Was Stalin Really Necessary?* (London: Geo. Allen and Unwin, 1964).

SUGGESTIONS FOR READING

Except for John Maynard Keynes' *General Theory* and Warren Nutter's article, which are for the initiated in economics, the books and articles cited in the footnotes to the Introductions are highly readable and rewarding. Some very readable, provocative, and incisive sections of the *General Theory* include pages 128–31, 147–164, 333–371 and 372–384.

Peter Wiles argues that allocational inefficiency is the price an economy has to pay for growing rapidly and that capitalist economies put excessive emphasis on consumers' choice thereby foregoing growth. The argument, stated eloquently in "Growth versus Choice," *Economic Journal* (June 1965), pp. 244–255, is restated at greater length in *The Political Economy of Communism* (Oxford, 1962).

Raymond Aaron attacks what he considers an obsession with economic growth in "The Growth Rate Fantasy," *The Radical Humanist* (Calcutta), Vol. XXVIII, No. 8 (Feb. 23, 1964).

Bertram M. Gross' "When Is a Plan Not a Plan," *Challenge* (Dec. 1961), and Gerhard Colm's "Economic Planning in the United States," *Weltwirtschaftliches Archiv* (March 1964) blur the boundaries between command and demand systems.

Deborah C. Paige with F. T. Blackby and S. Freund, "Economic Growth: The Last Hundred Years," *Economic Review* (July 1961), reprinted in Edmund S. Phelps, *The Goal of Economic Growth* (New York, 1962), pp. 69–89, is an excellent reference for eleven western countries. Alec Nove, "Prospects for Economic Growth in the USSR" *American Economic Review* (May 1963), pp. 541–55; Robert K. Campbell, "The Post War Growth in the Soviet Economy," *Soviet Studies* (July 1964), pp. 1–16; Gregory Grossman, "Thirty Years of Soviet Industrialization," *Dissent* (Spring 1959), pp. 150–60; and Alexander Eckstein, "Background of Soviet Economic Performance," in *The Soviet Economy*, ed. Morris Bornstein and Daniel R. Fusfeld (Homewood, Ill., 1963), pp. 3–12, together cover a half-century of Soviet growth in remarkable depth and lucidity. For comparisons of growth in income and productivity in the USSR and USA see *Economic Trends in the Soviet Union*, ed. Abram Bergson and Simon Kugnets (Cambridge, Mass., 1963), esp. pp. 12–16, 27–35. Josef Goldmann of Prague's Academy of Sciences argues that the Russian type of planning is causing fluctuations in, and retardation of, the rate of growth of Eastern European economies; see "Fluctuations and Trend in the Rate of Economic Growth in Some Socialist Countries," *Economics of Planning*, Vol. 4, No. 202 (1964).

J. Marcus Fleming and Victor R. Sertic, "The Yugoslav Economic System," *IMF Staff Papers* (July 1962); Bela A. Balassa, *The Hungarian Experience with Economic Planning* (New Haven, 1959); Jan M. Michal, *Central Planning in Czechoslovakia* (Stanford, 1960); and John Michael Montias, *Central Planning in Poland* (New Haven, 1962), describe in detail some of the planned economies under communism, while the March 1964 issue (Vol. 92, No. 1) of *Weltwirtschaftliches Archiv* has papers on planning in the Netherlands, Japan, Norway, Great Britain, and other economies.

For an excellent description of what a competitive price system does and does not do well in a static context see R. A. Radford, "The Economic Organization of a P.O.W. Camp," *Economica*, Vol. XII, No. 48, New Series (Nov. 1945), pp. 189–201. That competition is efficient not only statically (in allocating resources) but also dynamically, is the theme of Ludwig Erhard's *Prosperity Through Competition* (New York, 1958), and of the German Economist Wilhelm Röpke, *A Humane Economy* (Chicago, 1960). Alesky Waksar and Janusz A. Zielinski, argue that a planned economy needs more than one set of prices for different purposes in "Socialist Operational Price Systems" in the *American Economic Review* (Dec. 1962), pp. 55–84. Harold Hallaroker has compiled and/or translated a good selection on "Soviet Discussion on Enterprise Incentives and Methods of Planning" in *Economics of Planning*, Vol. 3, No. 1 (Apr. 1963), pp. 53–68. Alec Nove assesses the impact of this debate in "The Changing Role of Soviet Prices," *ibid.* Vol. 3, No. 3 (Dec. 1963), pp. 185–195; also see Marshall I. Goldman, "Economic Controversy in the Soviet Union," *Foreign Affairs* (April 1963). *Time* magazine, "Borrowing from the Capitalists" (Feb. 12, 1965), reviewed this debate and especially the contribution of Russan economist Yevsei Liberman and concluded that the Soviet economy was moving towards capitalism. A different answer is given by the American economist Hans Apel in "Is Russian Planning Becoming More Capitalistic?" *Challenge* (June 1965).

Andrew Shonfield's "The Progress (and Perils) of Planning," *Encounter* (August 1965), pp. 32–41, is a timely stocktaking in view of the increasing popularity of planning discussed briefly by Theodore Geiger and John C. Honey in "National Economic Planning in Western Europe," *Looking Ahead* (June 1963), pp. 4–7.